Conversations with
Jimmy Carter

Literary Conversations Series
Monika Gehlawat
General Editor

Conversations with Jimmy Carter

Edited by Tom Head

University Press of Mississippi / Jackson

The University Press of Mississippi is the scholarly publishing agency of
the Mississippi Institutions of Higher Learning: Alcorn State University,
Delta State University, Jackson State University, Mississippi State University,
Mississippi University for Women, Mississippi Valley State University,
University of Mississippi, and University of Southern Mississippi.

www.upress.state.ms.us

The University Press of Mississippi is a member
of the Association of University Presses.

First printing 2023
∞

Library of Congress Cataloging-in-Publication Data

Names: Head, Tom, editor.
Title: Conversations with Jimmy Carter / edited by Tom Head.
Other titles: Literary conversations series.
Description: Jackson : University Press of Mississippi, [2023] | Series: Literary
    conversations series | Includes bibliographical references and index.
Identifiers: LCCN 2023006026 (print) | LCCN 2023006027 (ebook) |
    ISBN 9781496846228 (hardback) | ISBN 9781496846235 (trade paperback) |
    ISBN 9781496846242 (epub) | ISBN 9781496846259 (epub) |
    ISBN 9781496846266 (pdf) | ISBN 9781496846273 (pdf)
Subjects: LCSH: Carter, Jimmy, 1924—Interviews. | Presidents—United
    States—Interviews. | United States—Politics and government—1977–1981.
Classification: LCC E873 .C66 2023 (print) | LCC E873 (ebook) |
    DDC 973.926092—dc23/eng/20230313
LC record available at https://lccn.loc.gov/2023006026
LC ebook record available at https://lccn.loc.gov/2023006027

British Library Cataloging-in-Publication Data available

Books by Jimmy Carter

Why Not the Best? Nashville, TN: Baptist Sunday School Board, 1975.

A Government as Good as Its People. New York: Simon & Schuster, 1977.

Keeping Faith: Memoirs of a President. Fayetteville, AR: University of Arkansas Press, 1982.

Negotiation: The Alternative to Hostility. Macon, GA: Mercer University Press, 1984.

The Blood of Abraham: Insights into the Middle East. Chicago: Houghton Mifflin, 1985.

Everything to Gain: Making the Most of the Rest of Your Life (with Rosalynn Carter). New York: Random House, 1987.

Turning Point: A Candidate, a State, and a Nation Come of Age. New York: Three Rivers, 1992.

An Outdoor Journal: Adventures and Reflections. Fayetteville, AR: University of Arkansas Press, 1994.

Always a Reckoning, and Other Poems. New York: Times, 1995.

Talking Peace: A Vision for the Next Generation. Revised edition. New York: Dutton, 1995.

Living Faith. New York: Times, 1996.

Sources of Strength: Meditations on Scripture for a Living Faith. New York: Times, 1997.

The Virtues of Aging. New York: Ballantine, 1998.

An Hour Before Daylight: Memories of a Rural Boyhood. New York: Simon & Schuster, 2001.

Christmas in Plains: Memories. New York: Simon & Schuster, 2001.

The Nobel Peace Prize Lecture: Delivered in Oslo on the 10th of December, 2002. New York: Simon & Schuster, 2002.

The Hornet's Nest: A Novel of the Revolutionary War. New York: Simon & Schuster, 2003.

Sharing Good Times. New York: Simon & Schuster, 2004.

Our Endangered Values: America's Moral Crisis. New York: Simon & Schuster, 2005.

Palestine: Peace Not Apartheid. New York: Simon & Schuster, 2006.

Beyond the White House. New York: Simon & Schuster, 2007.

A Remarkable Mother. New York: Simon & Schuster, 2008.

We Can Have Peace in the Holy Land: A Plan That Will Work. New York: Simon & Schuster, 2009.

White House Diary. New York: Farrar, Straus, and Giroux, 2010.

Through the Year with Jimmy Carter: 366 Daily Meditations from the 39th President. Grand Rapids, MI: Zondervan, 2011.

A Call to Action: Women, Religion, Violence, and Power. New York: Simon & Schuster, 2014.

The Little Baby Snoogle-Fleejer (with illustrations by Amy Carter). Fayetteville, AR: University of Arkansas Press, 2014.

A Full Life: Reflections at Ninety. New York: Simon & Schuster, 2015.

Faith: A Journey for All. New York: Simon & Schuster, 2018.

Contents

Introduction

Jimmy Carter wasn't the first president of the television era, but it could be argued that he was the first president whose tenure was defined by television coverage. Richard Nixon had achieved national prominence as Eisenhower's vice president; John F. Kennedy and Lyndon Johnson were as much creatures of radio as they were of television. But by Carter's time, television news had reached peak influence. Nielsen data from 1974 indicated that the average American household spent more than six hours each day watching TV,[1] and widespread Internet usage was still more than twenty years away. Television news, fresh off the heels of its coverage of Watergate and the Vietnam War, had never been more credible or more influential. It would have been a perfect time for a slick, well-packaged presidential candidate with Hollywood credentials to conquer national politics, which is what happened in 1980.

But what the American public got in 1976, and fell in love with, was a family-minded, ex-military Georgia peanut farmer who went to a Baptist church and wore blue jeans to media events. Governor Carter wasn't an innocent political outsider, of course; he had already navigated the choppy waters of Georgia's tense, liminally segregationist politics as a racial moderate in the aftermath of Lester Maddox's success. This took considerable sophistication and endurance, a mix of undeniable authenticity and plausibly deniable brand savvy. When he brought these traits to the bleak post-Nixon presidential horserace, it was welcome and refreshing. There was not just a charisma but a power to this rural candidate, who seemed like a "creature raised up out of nowhere by his own will" (as *Newsweek* called him),[2] who didn't have to play by the same rules as his predecessors.

The two 1976 interviews in this volume, each remarkable in their own way, reflect that early period in Carter's career. The first interview with Bill Moyers was a much bigger deal at the time than audiences might realize today, as PBS was a national juggernaut with a massive viewing audience. Moyers, who served as press secretary under Johnson, had long since moved on to his vocation as a philosopher-journalist; his friendly but assertive interview of Carter delves deeply into religious and existential themes in a way that was already unusual then, and would certainly be unusual in today's more guarded political environment. Although the interview seems superficially friendly, Moyers would later tell historian Arthur Schlesinger Jr. that he assessed Carter the candidate as "cold, tough, [and] terrifyingly self-confident."[3] Moyers would come to revise this assessment by his second interview.

The latter of these two 1976 interviews, Robert Scheer's *Playboy* feature, was much more controversial. This is partly because it was *Playboy*, whose branding was almost as opposite that of Carter's as it would be possible for a magazine's branding to be. The presence of the wholesome and earthy Carter, talking about God and his upbringing between airbrushed centerfolds, is bizarre. Carter's candor, particularly his unprompted confession that he had felt lust for women other than his wife, made it all even stranger. Carter came to despise the experience, remarking on more than one occasion that it almost cost him the election.[4] But the interview is striking, not only because it was such a bizarre moment in American political history but also because of its exceptional content. This is rural evangelicalism in deep dialogue with urban secularism and, while he may have suffered politically for this dialogue, the conversation was a fruitful one that has much to say about not only Carter himself, but the world around him. It wasn't Carter's best moment, but it might have been *Playboy*'s best moment.

By the time Moyers and Carter reconnected in November 1978, his assessment of Carter had shifted to one that recognized his warmth and flexibility, but he saw within it all a liability. This may be reflected in the shifting tone of the questions, which centered less on bringing out his humanity and more on bringing out specificity on policy questions. Moyers is not rude to Carter, but he is skeptical; it's clear that the hopeful, optimistic tone of Carter's campaign has given way to the cynical realities of American politics, and it is possible to read both Moyers's frustration and Carter's within this interaction. Several months after this second interview, Moyers remarked that "political criticism centered on the absence of a clear White House position on a range of issues," that Carter "walks a high wire, juggling a multitude of special interests."[5] The fact that Moyers's 1976 and 1979 assessments differed so much speaks to the challenges Carter faced in national political life: not very many people, in the media or in Washington, seemed to know where he fit in once the novelty wore off.

From the Presidency to the Postpresidency

The long gap between the third and fourth interview reflects Carter's relative absence from public life following the 1980 election. Both the media and the national Democratic Party initially treated the ex-president as if he were a liability at best, a national embarrassment at worst. This assessment of Carter's presidency has softened over time. "I do think," Carter biographer Jonathan Alter recently remarked, "that historians are starting to recognize that [Carter] got slimed in some ways after he left office."[6] But this has been a four-decade process, and national media interest in Carter, and Carter's corresponding interest in the national media, was not especially high in the immediate aftermath of his presidency.

He found other ways to stay busy. The former president and his wife, Rosalynn, founded the Carter Center in 1982 and went right to work leveraging the connections they had made during his presidency into international diplomatic and humanitarian relief projects. In 1984 they began working with Habitat for Humanity, beginning a productive forty-year partnership. By the time of the fourth interview in this volume, a 1990 conversation with Vicki Quade titled "Jimmy Carter Works the World," Carter had established himself as a powerful human rights negotiator without portfolio whose work in eight countries had borne fruit and whose post-presidential vocation was beginning to take clearer shape. As a September 1989 cover story put it, following his then-recent efforts in Ethiopia and Nicaragua: "this quiet, 64-year-old statesman recently has emerged as a determined private diplomat, devoting his retirement to humanitarian efforts around the world."[7] The same could be said of how he was still spending his retirement thirty years later.

This isn't to say that Carter didn't still have strong political opinions, and we see some of this in this volume's fifth interview, his January 1993 *Fresh Air* interview with Terry Gross. Here he discusses his book *Turning Point* (1992), a personal history of the 1962 Georgia elections, and the ways in which Southern party bosses such as Joe Hurst had subverted democracy over the course of the nation's history. Carter was not a fan of emerging party leader Bill Clinton during the 1992 Democratic presidential nomination process and declined to endorse him at that time; he warmed up to the Clintons somewhat but was never one of their most convinced supporters, voting for Barack Obama over Hillary Clinton in the 2008 primary and Bernie Sanders in 2016. The interview with Gross provides some historical context on why Carter may have found the transactional political environment of the 1990s especially alienating, perhaps reminiscent of what he liked least about his own experiences with Southern politics.

The sixth interview, Shirin Sinnar's 1996 *Harvard International Review* conversation with Carter, focuses on his role as a foreign policy expert and third-party diplomatic mediator. The tone is more practical than academic, perhaps a reflection of Sinnar's own efforts as a scholar-practitioner in the areas of international law and human rights advocacy. She and Carter do sound, in this relatively brief interview, as if they are talking shop about the most constructive ways to reduce violence, conflict, and suffering in a complex world often resistant to their efforts.

An Elder in the New Century

At the beginning of the twenty-first century, Jimmy Carter found himself increasingly alienated from American political culture. His well-known evangelicalism had become tied to a political party, and the party wasn't his; George W. Bush, the second evangelical president of the modern era, applied principles similar to Carter's in a very different way. Further complicating matters was the decreasing popularity of peace efforts in the aftermath of the September 11 attacks. Carter still engaged this world in an active way but did not always find it very welcoming.

He returns to *Fresh Air* in the volume's seventh interview, where he focuses on the changing role of religion in American life, the abandonment of austerity and restraint as religious values, and the looming threat of climate change. Although the November 2005 interview has political overtones, it is not partisan; this reflects Carter's increasingly clear role as a post-partisan elder figure, something he would codify not long afterwards when he joined Nelson Mandela's international third-party mediation group, the Elders, in 2007.

Carter reckons with his US legacy and the nature of leadership in the eighth interview, a scholarly discussion with Texas A&M University's George C. Edwards III, published in the March 2008 issue of *Presidential Studies Quarterly*. In some ways this is the driest and most conventional of the ten interviews, but also substantive in a way that few interviews are. Using the presidency as a springboard, it becomes a broader conversation about the nature of leadership, the benefits and perils of delegation, and the importance of being willing to do unpopular things. This interview gives a good overview of Carter's ethical praxis not only as a politician, but also as an author, nonprofit leader, and diplomat. He brings somber self-criticism into the conversation; there is none of the ordinary slickness or casual narcissism that one expects to suffer through in an interview with a former head of state. His ninth interview, with British journalist Carole Cadwalladr, further develops this humble self-assessment of his life and legacy.

In the tenth and final interview of the volume, Carter spends a lengthy morning segment with Ted Simons of Arizona Public Radio discussing the aging process, his childhood and military life, and prospects for the world's future. It may be the humblest interview in a volume full of humble interviews, a recognition that at this point in his life he no longer has anything left to prove.

TH

Notes

1. Les Brown, "TV Notes: Who Watches Even More TV Than Americans?," *New York Times*, June 29, 1975.

2. Quoted in Erica J. Selfert, *The Politics of Authenticity in Presidential Campaigns, 1976–2008* (McFarland, 2014), p. 45.

3. Quoted in Eric Alterman, *The Cause* (New York: Penguin, 2013), p. 296.

4. In his September 2010 *New York Times* interview with Maureen Dowd, for example, he remarks that he "almost lost the election" after speaking to *Playboy*.

5. *Bill Moyers Journal*, February 12, 1979.

6. *PBS NewsHour*, April 7, 2021.

7. Tanya Barrientos, "Official Afterlife is Revival for Carter," *Detroit Free Press*, September 8, 1989.

Chronology

1924	Born on October 1 in Plains, Georgia, to James Earl Carter Sr. (1894–1953) and Bessie Lillian (née Gordy) Carter (1898–1983).
1943	Attends the US Naval Academy in Annapolis, Virginia.
1946	Marries Rosalynn Smith and adapts to Navy life in Virginia, and wherever stationed elsewhere.
1953	After his father's unexpected death, Carter leaves his Navy career and returns to Plains, Georgia, to manage the family business.
1955	Elected to the Sumter County School Board.
1962	Elected to the Georgia State Senate.
1966	Runs unsuccessfully for governor of Georgia, winning 20.89 percent of the vote in the Democratic primary but losing to notorious segregationist Lester Maddox.
1970	Runs again for governor of Georgia, this time successfully, defeating a field of candidates in the Democratic primary and winning 59.28 percent of the vote in the general election.
1974	Announces presidential candidacy.
1976	After winning the crowded Democratic presidential primaries, Carter defeats incumbent President Gerald Ford, carrying 297 electoral votes and a majority of the popular vote.
1977	President Carter signs the Panama Canal Treaty.
1978	President Carter hosts the Camp David Accords.
1979	President Carter oversees the formation of the US Department of Education.
1980	President Carter is defeated by Ronald Reagan.
1982	Founds the Carter Center with his wife Rosalynn.
1984	Begins his long-term relationship with Habitat for Humanity.
1990	Assists in monitoring national elections in Nicaragua.
1994	Carter visits Haiti and North Korea in efforts to deescalate tensions between the governments of both countries and the United States.
2002	Wins Nobel Peace Prize.

2007   Founding member of the Elders, an organization of international emeritus leaders established by Nelson Mandela.

2010   Carter negotiates the release of US traveler Aijalon Gomes in North Korea.

2015   Diagnosed with metastatic brain cancer, successfully treated later in the year using immunotherapy.

Conversations with
Jimmy Carter

Interview

Bill Moyers / 1976

From *USA: People and Politics*, Public Broadcasting Service, May 6, 1976.
© The American Presidency Project.

Bill Moyers: When you were growing up in that wooden clapboard house on that dusty road, spearing fish in your spare time, or netting fish in your spare time, did you ever think about being president?

Governor Jimmy Carter: No. I didn't have but one desire, aspiration that I can remember, and that is going to the Naval Academy. Nobody in my father's family had ever finished high school before I did, and to actually go to college, in itself, was a notable goal to establish in our family.

And my father was in World War I, in the army—I had a very favorite uncle who was in the navy—and we saw in those Depression years that the best opportunity for me to get a college education was to go to one of the service academies where the tuition would be free. And Annapolis was my goal all the time until I went off to it.

Moyers: No other boyhood aspirations, fantasies?

Carter: No, no. When I was five years old, if anyone had asked me— what are you going to do when you grow up? I would have said: I want to go to Annapolis.

Moyers: Is that right?

Carter: And it was a kind of all-obsessive thing.

Moyers: I've been intrigued as to why you almost suddenly gave up a military career and went back to Plains. You make a gesture at telling why in there, but there's something missing to me. Your father died. And you thought about his life, and you went back, but was there something else?

Carter: Well, up until that time, I guess I was a naval officer who enjoyed my work. I had the best jobs in the Navy. I put into commission, as a pre-commission crew chief, the first ship the Navy built after the Second

[World] War, and then I went in the first nuclear submarine program. You know, the choice jobs in the whole navy.

And then my father had terminal cancer, and I had to go home to be with him about the last month of his life. I hadn't seen him since I was about seventeen years old. This was ten, twelve years later.

And I had always wanted, I guess, ultimately to be the Chief of Naval Operations, which is, you know, it's top of the navy. But when I went back home to where I had lived and saw what my father's life meant—in the view of those who knew him best—his service on the school board, his working for a new hospital, his dealing with the education of farmers who bought seed and so forth from him, his life in the church and his life in politics. He'd just been elected to the legislature and served one year when he died.

Well, I could see then a pull on me that was almost irresistible to go back and resubmit my ties to my birthplace. My family and my wife's family have both lived right there in Plains, Georgia. The members of our family who were born in the 1700s—we never have moved anywhere—and I guess that was a strong pull, too, that I didn't detect at the time.

But I think I had a choice to make. Did I want to be the Chief of Naval Operations and devote my whole life to that one narrowly defined career, which was a good one, or did I want to go back and build a more diverse life with a lot of friends, permanence, stability, in a community, in a relationship, in the life of a whole group of people? And I chose the latter.

Moyers: Did you regret that, those last eleven years of your father's life? You had really not been in close touch with him.

Carter: Well, I would like, obviously, in retrospect, to have been more with my father. I never thought he would die so young. But I've never regretted a day that I served in the Navy. That was an opportunity for me that paid off. I had a chance to travel extensively. I read and studied everything from, you know, music, drama, art, classical music, and so forth. I stretched my mind and had a great challenge, and I never had any regret for a single day that I spent in the navy. I never regretted getting out a single day after I left.

Moyers: What do you think it did for you or to you? Did it stamp this discipline that everyone tells me about? This respect for authority?

Carter: Yes, I think so. Obviously, the Naval Academy is quite heavily disciplined. And a life on a ship—particularly as a junior officer—is a heavy discipline; to move into submarines is a heavier discipline. And then I met Rickover, who knew me as one of his maybe four young naval officers who had come in on the *Seawolf* and the *Nautilus*, which were the two submarines that were built with atomic power. And he demanded from me a standard of performance and a depth of commitment that I had never realized before that I could achieve. And I think second to my own father, Admiral Rickover had more effect on my life than any other man.

Moyers: What did he say to you? What was it? You reminded me of something Robert Penn Warren said to me in a recent conversation like this—he said, "I'm convinced now that the single most indispensable element in any human being's life is the touch of another individual who says, 'You matter. You make a difference.'"

And I was going to ask you, who's done that in your life, and you say it's your father and Rickover.

Carter: I said "men." Yes. Well, there was no personal interrelationship between me and Rickover. It was an impersonal demand of a perfectionist.

Moyers: Can you step back as the civilian commander in chief from this heavy influence of the military and of an admiral in your life?

Carter: I can.

Moyers: Can you?

Carter: Yes, yes. There's no aspect of a militaristic inclination now on my part. I feel free of that completely. But the self-discipline has stuck with me. I have a constant drive just to do the best I can, and sometimes it's disconcerting to other people, but it's not an unpleasant thing for me. I don't feel that I've got to win, or that I, you know, that I'll be terribly disappointed if I don't win. I feel a sense of equanimity about it. If I—if I do my best and lose, I don't have any regrets.

Moyers: What drives you?

Carter: [*Long silence*] I don't know [. . .] exactly how to express it. As I said, it's not an unpleasant sense of being driven. I feel like I have one life to live. I feel like that God wants me to do the best I can with it. And that's quite often my major prayer. Let me live my life so that it will be meaningful. And I enjoy attacking difficult problems and solving of solutions and answering the difficult questions and the meticulous organization of a complicated effort. It's a challenge—possibly it's like a game. I don't know. I don't want to lower it by saying it's just a "game," but it's an enjoyable thing for me.

Moyers: How do you know—this is a question I hear a lot of young people—how do you know God's will?

Carter: Well, I pray frequently. Not continually, but many times a day. When I have sense of peace and just self-assurance—I don't know where it comes from—that what I'm doing is the right thing, I assume, maybe in an unwarranted way, that that's doing God's will.

Moyers: Let's go back a minute to the people who touched you.

Carter: Yes.

Moyers: When you were young: who else?

Carter: Well, there were two women, in particular, when I was young. One, obviously, was my mother. I'm much more like my mother than I am my father. She read day and night, at the breakfast table, the lunch table, the supper table. I do, still. She was very compassionate.

Moyers: You mean she read out loud?

Carter: No, no. No; she just read books. And so did I, by the way. My father didn't. He read the newspaper and maybe *U.S. News & World Report*, and that was just about it. Mother always was a champion of disadvantaged people. In our area it was poor whites and all Blacks. Later, when she was past retirement age, she, as you know, went to India for two years, and she, I think, she came back when she was after seventy.

Moyers: The Peace Corps?

Carter: In the Peace Corps, yes. In the Peace Corps. But she's always been that way. Miss Julia Coleman was a superintendent of our school when I was growing up in Plains. Plains is a town of about 600 population. The schoolhouse is still there. And she saw something in me, I think, when I was a little child, a hunger to learn, and although I lived in a rural area, three or four miles, three miles from Plains. We didn't have electricity or running water. But we didn't suffer. But she made sure that I listened to classical music. She would make me do it. And she'd make sure that I learned the famous paintings and the artists, and she gave me lists of books to read, and she was very strict with me.

Moyers: Who were the villains in your life?

Carter: Well, I never had any really any traumatic experiences. I never had any overwhelming fears or deprivations. I lived a sheltered life. My mom and my daddy were always there. And we lived in an isolated area. There were about two white families and maybe twenty-five or thirty Black families around. The dominant family in the community was a Black family, an AME bishop, Bishop Johnson.

But when things went wrong, you know, in the field or in the woods or in school, home was always a haven. So I never did have any fears, I guess, no villains that I can think of.

Moyers: You said once that you never really seriously considered disobeying your father. And I wonder if anyone who never disobeyed his father can understand the rest of us.

Carter: [*Laughter*] Well, as a matter of fact, I never disobeyed my father in that when he said, "Jimmy, you do something," I failed to do it. But on many occasions I did things that I knew my father didn't like, and I was punished very severely because of it.

In fact, my father very seldom gave me an order. If all the other field workers were off for the afternoon, and he wanted me to turn the potato vines so they could be plowed Monday morning, Daddy would say to me—he called me "Hot."

Moyers: He called you what?

Carter: "Hot"—"Hot Shot"—is what he called me. He says, "Hot, would you like to turn the potato vines this afternoon?" And I would much rather go to the movies or something. But I always said, "Yes, sir, Daddy, I would." And I would do it. But he didn't have to give me many direct orders. But I never did disobey a direct order my father gave me.

Moyers: You wanted to be a good boy?

Carter: Well, it wasn't a namby-pamby sort of thing. My father was my friend. And I respected him. I never said "yes" or "no" to my father. I would say, "yes, sir," "no, sir," to my mother, too, still do, and to most people that I don't know well. But it was a matter of respect. It wasn't any matter of trying to kow-tow to him or . . .

Moyers: Was a stern life?

Carter: I—I . . .

Moyers: I grew up on the Meridian about 500, oh, 400 miles due west from you. We danced not at all. We never went to a movie on Sunday. One of the first spankings I got was when I went—slipped off and went to a movie on Sunday. We had to go to BTU, and if we violated it, we were in trouble. It was a stern life. Was it in Plains?

Carter: Yes; it was a stern life. But there wasn't much to do. [*Laughter*] If it hadn't been a stern life—we didn't have any movies in Plains, and I remember that when I was a small child, we had a very small bowling alley that was not nearly as long as a regular one was, but it was an exciting thing for Plains when we had a bowling alley for a while, with the small balls.

But my life was spent in a fairly isolated way, out in the woods and in the streams and swamps and fields. My classmates were—my playmates were Black—my classmates were white. And my whole environment was completely rural. Plains was the nearest town, population of 600. And I only went there when I had to. I did attend school there, and [. . .] it was a growing factor in my life, but my background is all in the woods.

Moyers: What do you do now for fun?

Carter: I read a lot, and I have a—about the only thing that I do for fun now is to look forward to being home. I stay gone a lot, away from Plains, away from our house, away from our little daughter, away from my wife, away from my mother, away from my mother-in-law, my brother, and sisters and my wife's kinfolks. And when I get home, I change immediately into work clothes, put on brogans and dungarees, and either go to the farm or walk in the woods. My wife and I hunt arrowheads. We go out into the fields after they've been plowed and rained on, and we walk sometimes for hours, just talking to each other about different things, sometimes politics, quite often about our family. We have very few moments alone. And so the fun in my life is just reestablishing for a twenty-four or thirty-two-hour period, whatever it is, the structure of my family.

Moyers: What do you think you're on earth for?

Carter: I don't know. I could quote the Biblical references to creation, that God created us in his own image, hoping that we'd be perfect, and we turned out to be not perfect but very sinful. And then when Christ was asked what are the two great commandments from God which should direct our lives, he said, "To love God with all your heart and soul and mind, and love your neighbor as yourself." So I try to take that condensation of the Christian theology and let it be something through which I search for a meaningful existence. I don't worry about it too much anymore. I used to when I was a college sophomore, and we used to debate for hours and hours about why we're here, who made us, where shall we go, what's our purpose.

But I don't feel frustrated about it. You know, I'm not afraid to see my life ended. I feel like every day is meaningful. I don't have any fear at all of death. I feel like I'm doing the best I can, and if I get elected president, I'll have a chance to magnify my own influence, maybe in a meaningful way. If I don't get elected president, I'll go back to Plains. So I feel like a sense of equanimity about it. But what—why we're here on earth, I don't know. I'd like to hear your views on that subject. [*Laughter*]

Moyers: Do you ever have any doubts? People say to me, "Jimmy Carter appears to be so full of certainty and conviction in a time when, as Gabriel said in Green Pastures, 'Everything that's loose is coming, everything that's tied together is turning loose, coming loose.'" Do you ever have any doubts? About yourself, about God, about life?

Carter: I can't think of any, you know. Obviously, I don't know all of the answers to the philosophical questions and theological questions that—you know, the questions that are contrived. But the things that I haven't been able to answer in a theory of supposition, I just accept them and go on. The things that I can't influence or change.

I do have, obviously, many doubts about the best way to answer a question or how to alleviate a concern or how to meet a need.

Moyers: I ran into a—by accident—into a friend of mine who's a lawyer in a large firm in New York, and this may have something to do with the origin of the question. He asked me where I was going when he saw me leaving, and I told him where I was coming down to, to do this conversation, and he said, "Could I ask you to ask Jimmy Carter something?" And I said, "Well, I'll try." And I wrote it down. He said: "What bothers me about Jimmy Carter, the human being, is that he strikes me as a decent but provincial and narrow-minded man from the South who's lived most of his life in that environment. And I'd like to know how a man like that expects to lead a pluralistic society, not to mention the Western world." And I said I would ask that. [*Laughter*]

Carter: OK, that's a good question. I'm not sure that you have to have lived in many different places to understand a pluralistic society. I've had a changing career myself. I started out as an isolated farmboy living in—as a minority member—in a predominantly Black neighborhood. I moved from that to a smaller town and then from there to a junior college—from there to Georgia Tech and then to the Naval Academy.

I've traveled extensively in foreign countries all my adult life. In the last four or five years, I've moved in foreign affairs on the level with prime ministers and presidents, foreign ministers, defense chiefs and so forth, as a governor.

For instance, when I've been to Israel, I've been with Mrs. Meir, Mr. Rabin, and Mr. Allon—and Mr. Rabin and others, and Mr. Eban. When I've been to Japan, I've been with Mr. Miki, Mr. Tanaka, Mr. Yokura, and Mr. Hohita [Ohira]. And I've been to Colombia; I've been with the president of Colombia. So I had a chance to learn [. . .] as a very eager student the possible ways to improve our interrelationships with those countries, talking to their leaders.

I've read extensively in the history of our country, the purpose of the president, the interrelationship between the president and the congress, about every one of the 435 congressional districts in this country, their demographic makeup, past voting records, primary interests of the people who live there. I've studied the campaign platform of every person who's ever run for president, whether they lost or won. And I've had a chance, as governor, to deal with a multiplicity of problems from different kinds of people, those who are mentally afflicted, those who are very rich and want favors, those who are corporate giants—they want to preserve a special privilege—those who are consumers and are hungry for a chance at the marketplace, those who are poor and illiterate, who are looking and not finding, criminal justice. So I think the diversity of my experience helps alleviate that. In my own career, life, I've been a farmer at first, and still am now, a businessman in a business I built fairly much myself, an engineer, a scientist, a naval officer, local and state government official. So I've had a broad background. That doesn't mean that I'm completely at home with all elements of a pluralistic society, but I think my background would be equivalent to many people who have become president, who have served successfully.

Moyers: What do you think of the three or four lessons that we have to take away from this last decade, if we don't get into trouble again?

Carter: One is to strip away secrecy of government in every possible way we can, to open up the deliberations of the executive and legislative branches of government.

Moyers: Would you let the minutes of the cabinet meeting be made public?

Carter: There would have to be some exclusions. States have done this. I'll get back to your question specifically in a minute. Florida, Georgia, Arkansas, California, and Massachusetts recently have done this. There have to be some exclusions.

When you have staff members advising a superior, that ought to be an area that would be kept private because you've got to have the freedom of debate and the chance for some inferior person in an organization to make a ridiculous suggestion and not be embarrassed later, from that same person a superior suggestion that might be put forward in a tentative way. It wouldn't be if he knew all the rough data was going to be spread in the public at a later time.

Moyers: All right, strip away secrecy.

Carter: Yes, strip away secrecy. The second thing is to make sure that we have, in our government, an access of the people in other ways. I would like to see, for instance, cabinet members go before joint sessions of Congress to be examined and questioned about foreign affairs, defense, agriculture, and so forth.

Moyers: Like the British system?

Carter: Yes. I would like to see that.

Moyers: You would send your secretary of state up to a joint session of Congress to actually answer questions from the floor?

Carter: Yes. I would. If the Congress would accept this, I will be glad to have it done.

The president ought to tell the truth always. I see no reason for the president to lie, and if any of my cabinet members ever lie, they'll be gone the next day.

Moyers: Governor, when you say that, when you say, "I will never lie, I will never mislead you," people have more doubts about your perception of reality than they do about your integrity.

Carter: I understand.

Moyers: Other people are now saying, "Jimmy Carter is trying to put one over on us. But Jimmy Carter just doesn't understand the way Washington international power works."

Carter: I understand that. And I have thought about that a lot, because I've been in debate a lot, and one of the great surprises to me in the campaign was that when I made that simple statement eighteen months ago—not in a fervent way, not even in a way to surprise anybody—that I, as a candidate and as a president, I'm not going to lie to you, that it became so controversial.

Moyers: Why were you surprised?

Carter: I was surprised that it was a controversy. The first time I ever voted was in 1948. I was in submarine school. All the other officers there voted for Dewey. I voted for Truman. He's still my favorite president. I don't believe that Truman ever told me a lie or told the American people a lie. He may have, but I don't believe he did. I think other presidents since then have. I don't see any reason for it.

Moyers: But doesn't this . . .

Carter: To me, that's important.

Moyers: Yes, yes; I can see that. But doesn't this go back to what the lawyer was saying earlier? Jimmy Carter's a nice man, but he doesn't really know that the world isn't a Christian place, that the world isn't a good place. The world is full of power brokers and power seekers, and people want things.

Carter: That may be true. But, as you know, Christians don't have a monopoly on the truth, and when I go out of office, if I'm elected, at the end of four years or eight years, I hope people will say, "You know, Jimmy Carter made a lot of mistakes, but he never told me a lie."

Moyers: If anybody came forward with the evidence in this campaign that you had lied, would you quit?

Carter: I think I would, because I haven't told a lie.

Moyers: If anybody came forward with evidence that while you were in the White House that you had lied, would you resign?

Carter: Well, I can't say that. But there will be times when I'm asked a question that I might refuse to answer. But if I give an answer, it will be the truth.

I think we ought to also have—I've forgotten the original question . . .

Moyers: The question was, what are the three or four lessons we musn't forget from the last ten years if we don't make the same mistakes. You said strip away secrecy.

Carter: I would never again—

Moyers: Tell me the truth.

Carter: [*Continuing*] Get militarily involved in the internal affairs of another country. Unless our own security is directly threatened.

Moyers: If North Korea invaded South Korea, would you get involved?

Carter: Well, we're already involved there. And we have a commitment by the Congress, the president, the people and the United Nations in South Korea. I would prefer to withdraw all of our troops and land forces from South Korea over a period of years—three, four years, whatever. But, obviously, we're already committed in Japan. We're committed in Germany.

Moyers: Well, where then does the Carter Doctrine apply?

Carter: Well, it would apply in retrospect to South Vietnam. It would apply in recent months to the attempt in Angola. It would apply possibly in the future in a place like Rhodesia. I just wouldn't do it. I don't think the American people need it. We don't have to show that we're strong. We are strong. And I wouldn't get involved militarily.

Another thing we must do in this country is to make the government mechanism work. It's an ineffective, bloated, confused, unmanageable bureaucracy there. And it—it hurts our people worse than anything I can think of almost—even compared to integrity in government, the competence of government is missing.

Moyers: Is that your vision? You open your autobiography by saying, "As we observe the 200th birthday of our nation, it's appropriate to ask ourselves two basic questions: One, can our government be honest, decent, open, fair and compassionate? Two, can our government be competent?"

Carter: That's right.

Moyers: Is that Jimmy Carter's vision for America—efficient government? Good government?

Carter: Good and efficient government. As far as the management of government, yes.

Moyers: I read your proposals and the record of your administration in Georgia on that—and I've read a lot of your speeches and analyses—the effect of which, it seems to me, is to centralize the executive branch of the government. It's to bring the power of the executive branch of government to bear through the White House. Don't you find people wary of centralized authority after the Lyndon Johnson administration and the war in Vietnam and Richard Nixon and Watergate?

Carter: No.

Moyers: You don't find people wary?

Carter: No, not of what you just described. When you say—when you throw Johnson, Watergate, Vietnam in the question, obviously, people are very wary about that.

Moyers: Right.

Carter: [*Laughs*] But I was trying to separate the subject and the predicate from all the other clauses that you added on to. They're all wary about what occurred with Watergate, with Vietnam, with the CIA, with Johnson, with Nixon—of course, they are. But it's not the fact that the government is well organized, managed, a clear delineation of authorities and responsibilities. I did it in Georgia, and not only did we save a lot of money and make it more economical and efficient—that was to some degree important—but the main thing is we opened up government so the people could understand it and control it.

It needs to be so that people who do jobs in the federal government— at all levels, from the bottom all the way up to the top—know what they're supposed to do. A clear delineation of authority; a chance for civil service employees to use whatever talent or ability or profession they have in a more productive way. To give service to our people; to minimize red tape, to mini- mize confusion, to minimize paperwork—just to let the government work.

Moyers: You're saying, in effect, "Trust me. I will do those things."

Carter: Yes.

Moyers: Is that right?

Carter: Yes.

Moyers: And there's no question but that you have tapped a feeling in the country that wants to trust.

Carter: Yes.

Moyers: Yet, in 1964 and 1965 and 1966, Lyndon Johnson said, "I have the facts. Trust me." In 1968, Richard Nixon said, "I have a secret plan to end the war in Vietnam. Trust me." Now, why, after two times burned, should the American people take from another politician the admonition, "trust me"?

Carter: Well, you know, I can't answer that question. There's a matter that I've already discussed—the absence of secrecy and truth. The only way

I know to restore the trust of the American people in the government is for the government to be trustworthy.

Moyers: Well, what does that mean? What would you—openness and, ah . . .?

Carter: I think openness and honesty. And truthfulness.

Moyers: Are you aware that once you become president, you will be making decisions that will immediately make some people unhappy who thought they saw in you a champion? Isn't that inevitable?

Carter: Yes.

Moyers: Well, what do you do about that disillusionment? And don't they then say, "Well, Jimmy Carter's not trustworthy?"

Carter: I can't answer that question. I think that we obviously went through this in Georgia. I laid down a whole thing, a series of things, that I promised to people. I campaigned four years. I wanted to be governor, didn't intend to lose. My wife and I shook hands with over 600,000 people. When I was elected, I very carefully had kept a list of everything I had promised. I was quite reticent—I carried all the promises. The legislature was not for me to begin with. They had thought my opponent was going to win. I won. And I cooperated with them. We did what I promised. I don't think I disillusioned the people of Georgia. I don't think Georgia is a disillusioned state now.

The ones who cling to me as a friend are the ones who throughout their whole lives have been deprived of an opportunity to make decisions about their own lives. I saw clearly as governor of Georgia, I see clearly now as a prospective, possible president, that in almost every instance, people who make decisions in government that affect human beings very seldom suffer when their decisions are wrong. The people who carved out a disgraceful, wasteful, confused, overlapping welfare system, their families never draw welfare. The people who carved out a disgraceful tax system, they don't ever get hurt because they're cared for when the tax laws are written.

The criminal justice system—I'm not a lawyer. We pride ourselves in having a good, fair criminal justice system. It's not fair. Now, wealth is a major factor in whether or not you get justice or not.

Moyers: That brings up the quote that you use in the beginning of your autobiography from someone we both admire—Reinhold Niebuhr—"The sad duty of politics is to establish justice in a sinful world." Do you think this is a just society?

Carter: No, no. I don't. I think one of the major responsibilities I have as a leader and as a potential leader is to try to establish justice. And that applies to a broad gamut of things—international affairs, peace, equality, elimination of injustice in racial discrimination, elimination of injustice in tax programs, elimination of injustice in our criminal justice system, and so forth. And it's not a crusade. It's just common sense.

Moyers: You're going to be an activist government?

Carter: I am.

Moyers: . . . President?

Carter: That's right.

Moyers: The profile that emerges is of a man who's into everything and pushing and pressing. How does that square with the reports we're getting of an antigovernment, anti-Washington mood in the country which you seem to represent?

Carter: I've never expressed deliberately any anti-Washington feeling or any antigovernment feeling. When, as Truman said, you know, people say I'm giving them hell, but when I tell the truth they think truth is hell. You know. I'm not going to disrupt anything when I get here to Washington, if I'm elected. I'm not anti-Washington at all. There's no one that I can think of that I would admit that cares more about my government than I do and who's thought about it more, studied it more and wants to see it run well more, wants to see it returned to the control of the people more. And when I come here, I think I'll get along fine. But I would be a very activist president. I never have said I wanted a small government. I want one that, when it performs a function, does it well and performs a function in the ways that alleviate the problems of those who have not had an adequate voice in the past.

Moyers: What do you think the purpose of government is?

Carter: To provide legitimate services to our people; to help preserve peace; to provide a mechanism by which the people's character can be expressed in international affairs. I think the purpose of government is to alleviate inequities. I think the purpose of government is to provide for things that we can't provide ourselves.

Moyers: How do you see the presidency, for example? What's the purpose of the president?

Carter: Well, of course, a president has a many-faceted character. As does an individual. And does a nation.

I think the major thing that I study about is the relationship between the president and the Congress and the function of a president as he relates to the people. And maybe that's the question that you're asking. And the kind of president that we need.

I think the president ought to be—I think the nation's best served by a president who is strong and aggressive and innovative and sensitive. Working with the Congress. Is strong, independent, in harmony for a change, with mutual respect for a change. In the open, and with a minimum of secrecy for a change. I don't think the Congress is capable of leadership. That's no reflection on the Congress, but you can't have 535 people leading the nation. I don't think the Founding Fathers ever thought that Congress would lead this country.

There's only one person in this nation that can speak with a clear voice to the American people. There's only one person that can set a standard of ethics and morality and excellence and greatness or call on the American people to make a sacrifice and explain the purpose of the sacrifice, or answer difficult questions or propose and carry out bold programs, or to provide for defense posture that would make us feel secure, a foreign policy that would make us proud once again, and that's the president. In the absence of that leadership, there is no leadership, and the country drifts.

So a strong president, yes. But an autocratic president, an imperial presidency, no.

Moyers: You think that day is over?

Carter: Yes, it's over. But I think the only way to guarantee it—against it is to remove the tight secrecy that binds around someone once they've started making a serious mistake. We've had some presidents that were incapable of admitting, "Look, I've made a mistake." And that's been the cause of a great deal of our woe in this country in the last number of years, as you know. Other presidents said, "Look, I messed up on that one. This is what happened. I was at fault. This is—the people who were culpable. We've corrected it. It won't happen again."

But that freedom with the people, and the absence of the need to constantly prove oneself as being superior, is an important personal characteristic in a president. I think it would prevent another Vietnam or another Watergate.

Moyers: Let me go back to some personal questions as we close here. You said once that you were strongly influenced by a sermon whose title was "If You Were Arrested for Being a Christian, Would There Be Enough Evidence to Convict You?" What is the evidence that the rest of us can see of a Christian?

Carter: [*Sigh*] I don't know. That's a hard question to answer, because I don't think I'm better than anyone else. I reckon there's my own shortcomings and sinfulness and need to improve, and need for forgiveness among the people around me and God.

I was going through a state in my life then that was a very difficult one. I had run for governor and lost. Everything I did was not gratifying. When I succeeded in something, it was a horrible experience for me. And I thought I was a good Christian. I was the chairman of the Board of Deacons. I was the head of the brotherhood in all the thirty-four churches in my district, and head of the finance committee, and a Sunday school teacher just about all my life. I thought I really was a great Christian.

And one day the preacher gave this sermon—I don't remember a thing he said—I just remember the title which you described—"If You Were Arrested for Being a Christian, Would There Be Any Evidence to Convict You?"

And my answer by the time that sermon was over was "No." I never had really committed myself totally to God—my Christian beliefs were superficial. Based primarily on pride, and—I'd never done much for other people. I was always thinking about myself, and I changed somewhat for the better. I formed a much more intimate relationship with Christ. And since then, I've had just about like a new life. As far as hatreds, frustrations, I feel at ease with myself. And it doesn't mean that I'm better, but I'm better off myself.

Moyers: Do you remember writing that—you were on a submarine, I believe, a submarine in the North Atlantic—when you heard that President Truman had dropped the atomic bomb on Hiroshima and Nagasaki, is that correct? You were [. . .] at sea?

Carter: I was at sea.

Moyers: Do you remember what you thought? And I'll come to the point in a minute. Do you remember what you thought when you heard that?

Carter: We were informed—I was at sea—the whole crew was informed that the president, President Truman, had a momentous announcement to make. We didn't know what it was going to be. The captain of the ship—maybe with orders over the radio—instructed all of us to gather before the loudspeaker systems on the ship. We thought that we had invaded Japan, and a lot of us young naval strategists had estimated how many people would be killed in this country. The generally accepted figure among us was a half million Americans would die as we captured Japan and ended the war.

Truman announced not that we had invaded Japan, but that a bomb of unprecedented power had been dropped on Japan. We had never heard of anything like this. It was a mystery to us. I didn't know obviously—have any concept of what was going on.

But I felt at that time a tremendous sense of relief that we had not, indeed, begun an invasion of Japan, and I can't remember now that long ago—

Moyers: Are you—

Carter: [*Continuing*] Other thoughts.

Moyers: Do you have the capacity to make that decision?

Carter: Yes, I believe so. I would use every resource in my life to prevent it. But I think I would have the capacity to make the choice between the lesser of two evils—and in my opinion, that was the kind of choice that Truman had to make. So, in a similar circumstance, the answer would be "Yes."

Moyers: Tom Ottenad, who's a very well-known writer for the *St. Louis Post Dispatch*—I see you know him—

Carter: Yes, I know him.

Moyers: [*Continuing*] Said recently, "In a ruthless business, Jimmy Carter is a ruthless operator. Even as he wears his broad smile and displays his southern charm." And the question that arises, and I've been inside the White House—I know some of the influences that work on a man trying to do the right thing—can you be ruthless in the way I think he means it here? And a Christian?

Carter: I presume—well, I'm a Christian, no matter what.

Moyers: But how do you reconcile?

Carter: Okay, he was talking about the campaign. And I don't know what he meant by "ruthless." I don't think I've ever deliberately hurt one of my opponents to gain an advantage. I try not to. I don't remember when I have. There may have been something that I've said in the heat of competition that made them feel discomforted. I can't deny that. But most people when they get to know me think that . . . finally decide that I'm much tougher than is originally apparent. So the word "ruthless" to me has connotations of cruelty. And I'm not sure I could be cruel.

Moyers: Let me ask it to you this way . . .

Carter: I think I can be tough in making decisions that were difficult. And I can be tenacious under difficult circumstances.

I have temptations to which I yield often. You know, to make compromises. One of the major criticisms of me by my opponents in the legislature, who've never yet been assuaged, is that I can't compromise. And that, that's a common criticism. I often had to compromise, but I didn't compromise in a back room. And didn't compromise to begin with. My preference was to spell out my position openly—this is what I propose; this is the reason for it; this is the mess we have now; this is what we can accomplish—try to work harmoniously with the legislature; try to give them all the credit they could, and then fight to the last vote. And I never was much able to get in a back room and compromise away the things I believed in.

And that's a very legitimate source of criticism for me. I'm not a good compromiser.

But I'll—I didn't suffer. I don't think Georgia suffered under my administration because of that attitude.

Moyers: I think what some people in this town are talking about is the unwillingness of Woodrow Wilson to compromise on the League of Nations.

Carter: Sure.

Moyers: The unwillingness of Lyndon Johnson to compromise on the war, or Richard Nixon on the opposition of the war, and a feeling that a disciplined, principled man, convicted of his own rightness, or having a private pipeline to God, in a sense, is going to say, "I'm right." And the town won't function because of his inability to compromise. Is that a legitimate danger?

Carter: I don't believe so. I can see that would be a legitimate concern, but I think the concern will be proven unjustified. They have a right to be concerned, but I don't think they need to be.

I'd like to quote one other thing—you've gotten into theology—Tillich said that religion is a search for the relationship between us and God and us and our fellow human beings. And he went on to say that when we quit searching, in effect, we've lost our religion. When we become self-satisfied, proud, sure, at that point we lose the self-searching, the humility, the subservience to God's will, the more intimate understanding of other people's needs, the more inclination to be accommodating, and, in that instant, we lose our religion.

So, the fact that a person has deep religious convictions doesn't necessarily mean that that person always thinks that he's right, that God's ordained him to take a dominant position. Although I have prayed a good bit, and do, I've never asked God to let me be president.

Moyers: Just to win the nomination?

Carter: I never—[*laughter*] I never asked God to let me win a single nomination. Never.

Moyers: What do you pray then?

Carter: I ask God to let me do what's right. And to let me do what's best—that my life be meaningful—in an optimum way, and, if I win or lose, I believe I can accept the decision with composure, and without regrets, or without animosities or hatreds, or deep disappointment even.

Moyers: In your own search for what Tillich said is the truth about man's relationship to man and to God?

Carter: Yes.

Moyers: What's the most significant discovery Jimmy Carter has made?

Carter: Well, I think I described it superficially a while ago. I think it affected my life more than anything else. This is embarrassing a little bit for me to talk about it, because it's personal, but in my relationship with Christ and with God, I became able in the process to look at it in practical terms, to accept defeat, to get pleasure out of successes, to be at peace with a world, and when I—for instance, one of the things that I derived from it in a—again in a kind of embarrassing way—is that when I stand on a factory shift line, like I did this morning in Erie, Pennsylvania, the General Electric plant, everybody that comes through there—when I shake hands with them, for that instant, I really care about them. In a genuine way. And I believe they know it. A lot of times.

Quite often I will shake hands with a woman who works in a plant, say, an older woman, and I'll just touch her hand, and quite frequently, they'll put their arms around my neck and say, you know, "God bless you, son." Or, "Good luck. I'll help you. Good luck." But it's kind of a relationship with people around me, but I don't want to insinuate that I'm better than other people. I've still got a long way to go, but you asked me a difficult question. What was the major discovery of my life? That's a hard thing to answer.

Moyers: But you care, though. You do—

Carter: I care.

Moyers: [*Continuing*] You have found that you care about people.

Carter: I do.

Moyers: Why not be a pastor or a bishop and not a president? [*Laughter*]

Carter: You've read my book. [*Laughter*] But this came up early in my life. You know, I got home from the navy, and I was thinking about running for the Georgia Senate—since some of you viewers haven't watched this, read the book—and we had a visiting pastor, and he was giving me a hard time about going into politics. He said it's a disgraceful profession, stay out of it. And I got angry, and I turned to him and kind of lashed back. I said, "How would you like to be a pastor of a church with some 80,000 members?" Because there were 80,000 people in this state senate district, I don't look on the presidency as a pastorate.

Moyers: I was going to ask you if the president—a pastor of 230 million.

Carter: No. Although Teddy Roosevelt said that it's a bully-pulpit, but, no . . . [*laughter*] . . . I don't look on it with religious connotations. But it gives me a chance to serve, and it also gives me a chance to magnify whatever influence I have—either for good or bad, and I hope it will be for the good.

Moyers: Gives you power, too.

Carter: And power . . .

Moyers: You have been searching for power for the last ten years.

Carter: I can't deny it.

Moyers: You did Georgia State Senate, and then you—

Carter: Sure.

Moyers: [*Continuing*] Ran four years for the governorship and been running two years for the presidency. Do you need power?

Carter: Well, I think so. That is an unfulfilled, all-obsessive hunger—no. I feel powerful enough now. And secure enough now. Wealthy enough now. I have a good family life now. I've got a lot of blessings that would give me a good life for the rest of my days. But I like to have a chance to change things that I don't like, and to correct the inequities as I discern them, and to be a strong spokesman for those that are not strong. And I guess that's power. So, I can't deny that one of the purposes that I want to be president is to have power, yes.

Moyers: One final question. If we learned anything the last few years, it has been that good intentions in the use of great power are no guarantee that that power will be used wisely.

Carter: That's right.

Moyers: That the character of the man is less important to the safeguards against the abuse of power than the checks and balances on the office and on the power.

Carter: I understand that.

Moyers: And here Jimmy Carter is coming along saying, "I want to do all these things because I believe they're right. I want more power because I want to do good things. And trust me, I won't abuse the power."

Now, after the last ten years, why should someone believe you? They may trust you. They may know that you are sincere and well-intentioned, and yet they know it is power that often changes the man, and not the man who changes power.

Carter: I know. I can see that. That's why I go back to what I said originally. You need to have an open government. You need to tell the truth. A minimum of secrecy. Let the people have a maximum part of play in the evolution and consummation of our domestic and foreign policies. That gives you a safety net under an incompetent or distorted president—the people themselves. And I think had we told the people the truth about Vietnam, we would have been out very early. Had the people had the truth about Watergate, it would never have happened.

Moyers: So you're saying Jimmy Carter's character is not enough.

Carter: That's right.

Moyers: You want checks. You want balances. You want safeguards.

Carter: I don't object to those. I don't object to a strong, aggressive Congress. A strong, aggressive Supreme Court. And a strong, aggressive president—if what goes on in our government is known by, debated by, questioned by, controlled by the people of this country.

Now, I can see that there are times when an inspirational leader can actually elevate the people. That may happen on rare occasions. I think for a while, at least, John Kennedy did it. Roosevelt did it. This is a part of the presidency. There are times when the presidency, perhaps the government itself, might tend to sink below the standards, accumulatively speaking, of the people of this country—in which case, people support or boost that official or those officials in a weak moment. But to exclude the people completely, as we have tended to do in recent years, removes that common-sense judgment, character, safety that can preserve our country.

And it also destroys the concept of our government which did say that the government ought to be controlled by the people—and not by a powerful, secret, hidden, isolated, mistaken president. I don't want to see that ever happen again in this country. And I'd like to set the kind of tone, and perhaps the kind of laws, that would prevent a recurrence of these things, if that's humanly possible.

Moyers: What do you want for your children that you didn't have?

Carter: Well, I have to say that I had almost everything that I would have needed. I worked hard when I was a little child, but I'm proud of it. I lived in an isolated area when I was a little child, but I don't regret it now. I think those travels through the fields and swamps were, in retrospect, very precious days for me. So I would like to see what they already have—a much greater awareness of the world structure.

My eight-year-old daughter now knows more about biology and science and history and politics and foreign affairs than I did when I went off to college. And it's because she has television. She reads constantly. And because we educate her well, and, you know, we focus into her what we've learned. So each generation has a chance to be better. As far as knowledge is concerned. But also, they've lost something.

Moyers: Lost something?

Carter: Yes. Did I mention earlier, I think, in our conversation? I had a stability there, you know. When things started going wrong in my own life, my father and mother were there, and my sisters and brothers were there. And my church was there. And my community was there—that never did change. Never has changed yet. [*Laughs*] But there was something there around which I built my life.

In the modern-day world, you don't have that. It's a mobile world, and things to cling to are kind of scarce and few and far between. And which one of those advantages and disadvantages is the greater? I don't know. I wouldn't swap the life I had for the new, modern, fast-moving, open, nonstructured, minimal family life. But there are advantages now: knowing more earlier, traveling more, having a tighter interrelationship with your own peer group than I had. But which is best, I don't know. But maybe we could go back to some of those old principles which we knew when we went to BYPU on Sunday afternoon—[*laughter*]—and at the same time keep the advantages of a modem world. I'm sure we can keep the advantages of the modem world, but going back to those principles that give stability—of things that we're searching for. We haven't found them yet.

Moyers: I better explain to people that BYPU means Baptist Young People's Union.

Carter: Exactly.

Moyers: What was your favorite Baptist hymn?

Carter: Well, "Amazing Grace"—still is. It's "Amazing Grace."

Moyers: Thank you, Governor Carter.

Carter: Thank you.

The *Playboy* Interview with Jimmy Carter

Robert Scheer / 1976

Playboy, November 1, 1976. © 1976 Playboy. Reprinted by permission.

The biographical details are all too familiar by now and, indeed, may seem a little pointless this month. If Jimmy Carter is elected president of the United States a few weeks from now, the facts about where he spent his youth, how he was educated and the way he came out of nowhere to capture the Democratic nomination will soon enough be available in history books and on cereal boxes.

What will be less available and less familiar is what kind of person Carter is. To many Americans, the old charge that he was "fuzzy" on the issues may be less accurate than the persistent feeling that he is fuzzy as a personality. Even this late in the campaign, Carter remains for many an unknown quantity.

When Carter agreed to do a *Playboy* interview we decided we'd try our best not to add to all the hype that always gushes forth during a presidential campaign. We wanted to pit him against an interviewer who would prod him and challenge him and not be afraid to ask irreverent questions. Our choice of interviewer was natural: Robert Scheer, the Bronx-born Berkeley-based journalist who in the past year has done interviews with California governor Jerry Brown for *Playboy* (which was widely regarded as the earliest and most thorough exposure of Brown's curious politics and beliefs) and with both William and Emily Harris for *New York Times* (which provided crucial evidence in the trial of Patty Hearst).

For three months, Scheer dogged the footsteps of the peanut farmer who would be president, scrambling aboard press planes, sleeping in motels, hanging out with the pack of journalists that grew in size as the campaign gathered momentum. With the support of Carter's young aides—notably, press secretary Jody Powell and campaign manager Hamilton

Jordan—Scheer and *Playboy* managed to log more hours of recorded conversations with the candidate than any other publication or news medium—a fact Carter joked about at the final session. After writing the accompanying article about his experiences and about Carter, a very exhausted Scheer filed this report:

"It was the day after the Democratic Convention in New York City Jody Powell was harried.

"'Listen, Scheer, I'm not going to kid you. Now that he's the nominee, I've got over 700 requests from all over the world for interviews. He's told me to cut back, but I've got a prior commitment to you guys and I'm going to honor it. So hop a plane down to his place in Plains. We'll just cut out an appointment with some future Secretary of State.'

"Jody keeps his sense of humor even when lies harried. I had already logged hours of tape with Carter under conditions that were never less than chaotic. Our conversations had started when his chances were shakier and his time slightly more available. But, as Jody had said, once he became the nominee, it was going to be even tougher.

"Some of our sessions were as short as half an hour on board the campaign plane, with the roar of engines and the pilot's announcements adding to the frenzy. *Playboy* and I both hung in there through the months, taking (and paying for) flights halfway across the country on the tentative promise of yet one more hurried chat. After all the baggage searches by the Secret Service and the many times I'd had to lurch up an airplane aisle, fumbling with my tape recorder, I was looking forward to a leisurely conversation with Carter at his home after the nomination.

"Earlier this year, when I was working on the interview with Governor Jerry Brown, my *Playboy* editor, Barry Golson, had joined me for the final sessions at the governor's office in Sacramento. It had produced interesting results—I, the aggressive Berkeley radical, Golson, the Eastern diplomatic Yalie. We felt the Mutt-and-Jeff technique would be valuable with Carter as well, so Golson and I traveled to Plains for the final session.

"Down in Plains, everything was normal. Brother Billy Carter was in his blue overalls, leaning against a storefront, drawling about this and that to one of the locals who hadn't been up to New York City for the big show. We drove past the Secret Service barricades, past daughter Amy's lemonade stand, and parked in front of the Carter home. As we entered the front door, the candidate, dressed in rumpled work clothes and dusty clodhoppers, was ushering out an impeccably dressed six-man contingent from *Reader's Digest.*

"As we said hello and sat down in his living room to adjust our tape recorders, I remarked to Carter that he must be in a puckish mood, talking to both the *Digest* and *Playboy* on the same afternoon. Carter flashed us every one of his teeth: 'Yeah, but you guys must have some kind of blackmail leverage on Jody. I've spent more time with you than with *Time*, *Newsweek*, and all the others combined.'

"It was a flattering opening shot, but probably more canny and less casual than it sounded. A week earlier, during the Democratic Convention, Golson had bumped into Jordan at a party in New York. Neither of them was entirely sober, and they discussed the interview. Golson said something about all the time Carter had spent with me. Jordan replied, 'We wouldn't do it if it weren't in our interest. It's your readers who are probably predisposed toward Jimmy—but they may not vote at all if they feel uneasy about him.'

"For me, the purpose of the questioning was not to get people to vote for or against the man but to push Carter on some of the vagueness he's wrapped himself in. We tried to get beyond the campaigner to some of the personal doubts and confusions—as well as the strengths—of the man himself. Throughout my months on the campaign trail, I found Carter impatient with social chitchat and eager for challenging questions. He is thin-skinned, as others have reported, and he'll glare at you if he doesn't like something you've asked. But he can take it as well as dish it out and, unlike many other politicians I've interviewed, he'll eventually respond directly to a question if you press him hard enough. The best evidence of this is contained in the final portion of the interview, an open and revealing monolog that occurred because we happened to ask him one last question on a topic about which he'd become impatient and frustrated.

"Oh, just incidentally, there's one bit of folklore about Jimmy Carter whose authenticity I can vouch for. When I've had a rough day, I've been known to toss down a drink or four, and I wondered what Carter did when he needed replenishment. I got my answer during one short session as I slipped into the plane seat next to him after he'd had a miserable day on the hustings. Between answers, he would gobble down handfuls of peanuts at about the same rate at which I drink. Different strokes, I thought."

Playboy: After nearly two years on the campaign trail, don't you feel a little numbed by the routine—for instance, having to give the same speech over and over?

Jimmy Carter: Sometimes. Once, when I was campaigning in the Florida primary, I made twelve speeches in one day. It was the worst day I ever had.

But I generally have tried to change the order of the speech and emphasize different things. Sometimes I abbreviate and sometimes I elaborate. Of twenty different parts in a speech, I might take seven or eight and change them around. It depends on the audience—Black people, Jewish people, Chicanos—and that gives me the ability to make speeches that aren't boring to myself.

Playboy: Every politician probably emphasizes different things to different audiences, but in your case, there's been a common criticism that you seem to have several faces, that you try to be all things to all people. How do you respond to that?

Carter: I can't make myself believe these are contrivances and subterfuges I've adopted to get votes. It may be, and I can't get myself to admit it, but what I want to do is to let people know how I stand on the issues as honestly as I can.

Playboy: If you feel you've been fully honest, why has the charge persisted that you're "fuzzy" on the issues?

Carter: It started during the primaries, when most of my opponents were members of Congress. When any question on an issue came up, they would say, "I'm for the Kennedy-Corman bill on health care, period, no matter what's in it." If the question was on employment, they would say, "I'm for the Humphrey-Hawkins bill, no matter what's in it." But those bills were constantly being amended! I'm just not able to do that. I have to understand what I'm talking about, and simplistic answers identifying my position with such-and-such a House bill are something I can't put forward. That's one reason I've been seen as fuzzy. Another is that I'm not an ideolog and my positions are not predictable. Without any criticism of McGovern, if the question had ever come up on abortion, you could pretty well anticipate what he was going to say. If it were amnesty, you could predict what McGovern was going to say about that. But I've tried to analyze each question individually; I've taken positions that to me are fair and rational, and sometimes my answers are complicated.

The third reason is that I wasn't a very vulnerable opponent for those who ran against me. Fuzziness was the only issue Congressman Udall, Senator Church—and others that are hard to remember now—could adopt in their campaigns against me. I think the drumming of that factor into the consciousness of the American voter obviously had some impact.

Playboy: Still, not everybody's sure whether you're a conservative in liberal clothing or vice versa. F. D. R., for instance, turned out to be something of a surprise to people who'd voted for him, because he hadn't seemed as progressive before he was elected as he turned out to be. Could you be a surprise that way?

Carter: I don't believe that's going to be the case. If you analyze the Democratic Party platform, you'll see that it's a very progressive, very liberal, very socially motivated platform. What sometimes surprises people is that I carry out my promises. People ask how a peanut farmer from the South who believes in balanced budgets and tough management of government can possibly give the country tax and welfare reform, or a national health program, or insist on equal rights for Blacks and women. Well, I'm going to do those things. I've promised them during the campaign, so I don't think there will be many people disappointed—or surprised—when I carry out those commitments as president.

Playboy: But isn't it true that you turned out to be more liberal as governor of Georgia than people who voted for you had any reason to suspect?

Carter: I don't really think so. No, the *Atlanta Constitution*, which was the source of all information about me, categorized me during the gubernatorial campaign as an ignorant, racist, backward, ultraconservative, red-necked South Georgia peanut farmer. Its candidate, Carl Sanders, the former governor, was characterized as an enlightened, progressive, well-educated, urbane, forceful, competent public official. I never agreed with the categorization that was made of me during the campaign. I was the same person before and after I became governor. I remember keeping a check list and every time I made a promise during the campaign, I wrote it down in a notebook. I believe I carried out every promise I made. I told several people during the campaign that one of the phrases I was going to use in my inaugural speech was that the time for racial discrimination was over. I wrote and made that speech.

The ultraconservatives in Georgia—who aren't supporting me now, by the way—voted for me because of their animosity toward Carl Sanders. I was the alternative to him. They never asked me, "Are you a racist or have you been a member of the Ku Klux Klan?" because they knew I wasn't and hadn't been. And yet, despite predictions early this year by the *Atlanta Constitution* that I couldn't get a majority of the primary vote in Georgia against Wallace, I received about 85 percent of the votes. So I don't think the Georgia people have the feeling I betrayed them.

Playboy: Considering what you've just said about the *Atlanta Constitution*, how do you feel about the media in general and about the job they do in covering the election issues?

Carter: There's still a tendency on the part of some members of the press to treat the South, you know, as a suspect nation. There are a few who think that since I am a Southern governor, I must be a secret racist or there's something in a closet somewhere that's going to be revealed to show my true colors. There's been a constant probing back ten, twelve years in my background, even as early as the first primaries. Nobody probed like that into the background of Udall or Bayh or other people. But I don't object to it particularly, I just recognize it.

[*The answer was broken off and, at a later session, Carter returned to the question of the press and its coverage of issues. This time he was tired, his head sunk far back into his airplane seat. The exchange occurred during one of the late primaries.*]

Issues? The local media are interested, all right, but the national news media have absolutely no interest in issues at all. Sometimes we freeze out the national media so we can open up press conferences to local people. At least we get questions from them—on timber management, on health care, on education. But the traveling press have zero interest in any issue unless it's a matter of making a mistake. What they're looking for is a forty-seven-second argument between me and another candidate or something like that. There's nobody in the back of this plane who would ask an issue question unless he thought he could trick me into some crazy statement.

I don't think I would ever take on the same frame of mind that Nixon or Johnson did—lying, cheating, and distorting the truth. I think my religious beliefs alone would prevent that from happening.

Playboy: One crazy statement you were supposed to have made was reported by Robert Shrum after he quit as your speechwriter earlier this year. He said he'd been in conversations with you when you made some slighting references to Jewish voters. What's your version of what happened?

Carter: Shrum dreamed up eight or ten conversations that never took place and nobody in the press ever asked me if they had occurred. The press just assumed that they had. I never talked to Shrum in private except for maybe a couple of minutes. If he had told the truth, if I had said all the things he claimed I had said, I wouldn't vote for *myself*.

When a poll came out early in the primaries that said I had a small proportion of the Jewish vote, I said, "Well, this is really a disappointment to me—we've worked so hard with the Jewish voters. But my pro-Israel stand won't change, even if I don't get a single Jewish vote; I guess we'll have to depend on non-Jews to put me in office." But Shrum treated it as if it were some kind of racist disavowal of Jews. Well, that's a kind of sleazy twisting of a conversation.

Playboy: While we're on the subject of the press, how do you feel about an issue that concerns the press itself—the right of journalists to keep their sources secret?

Carter: I would do everything I could to protect the secrecy of sources for the news media.

Playboy: Both the press *and* the public seem to have made an issue out of your Baptist beliefs. Why do you think this has happened?

Carter: I'm not unique. There are a lot of people in this country who have the same religious faith. It's not a mysterious or mystical or magical thing. But for those who don't know the feeling of someone who believes in Christ, who is aware of the presence of God, there is, I presume, a quizzical attitude toward it. But it's always been something I've discussed very frankly throughout my adult life.

Playboy: We've heard that you pray twenty-five times a day. Is that true?

Carter: I've never counted. I've forgotten who asked me that, but I'd say that on an eventful day, you know, it's something like that.

Playboy: When you say an eventful day, do you mean you pray as a kind of pause, to control your blood pressure and relax?

Carter: Well, yes. If something happens to me that is a little disconcerting, if I feel a trepidation, if a thought comes into my head of animosity or hatred toward someone, then I just kind of say a brief silent prayer. I don't ask for myself but just to let me understand what another's feelings might be. Going through a crowd, quite often people bring me a problem, and I pray that their needs might be met. A lot of times, I'll be in the back seat of a car and not know what kind of audience I'm going to face. I don't mean I'm terror-stricken, just that I don't know what to expect next. I'll pray then, but it's not something that's conscious or formal. It's just a part of my life.

Playboy: One reason some people might be quizzical is that you have a sister, Ruth, who is a faith healer. The association of politics with faith healing is an idea many find disconcerting.

Carter: I don't even know what political ideas Ruth has had, and for people to suggest I'm under the hold of a sister—or any other person—is a complete distortion of fact. I don't have any idea whether Ruth has supported Democrats or not, whereas the political views of my other sister, Gloria, are remarkably harmonious with mine.

Playboy: So you're closer to Gloria, who has described herself as a McGovern Democrat and rides motorcycles as a hobby?

Carter: I like them both. But in the past twenty or twenty-five years, I've been much closer to Gloria, because she lives next door to me, and Ruth lives in North Carolina. We hardly saw Ruth more than once a year at family get-togethers. What political attitudes Ruth has had, I have not the slightest idea. But my mother and Gloria and I have been very compatible. We supported Lyndon Johnson openly during the 1964 campaign, and my mother worked at the Johnson County headquarters, which was courageous, not an easy thing to do politically. She would come out of the Johnson headquarters and find her car smeared with soap and the antenna tied in a knot and ugly messages left on the front seat. When my young boys went to school, they were beaten. So Mother and Gloria and I, along with my Rosalynn, have had the same attitudes even when we were in a minority in Plains. But Ruth lives in a different world in North Carolina.

Playboy: Granting that you're not as close to your religious sister as is assumed, we still wonder how your religious beliefs would translate into political action. For instance, would you appoint judges who would be harsh or lenient toward victimless crimes—offenses such as drug use, adultery, sodomy, and homosexuality?

Carter: Committing adultery, according to the Bible—which I believe in—is a sin. For us to hate one another, for us to have sexual intercourse outside marriage, for us to engage in homosexual activities, for us to steal, for us to lie—all these are sins. But Jesus teaches us not to judge other people. We don't assume the role of judge and say to another human being, "You're condemned because you commit sins." All Christians, all of us, acknowledge that we are sinful and the judgment comes from God, not from another human being.

As governor of Georgia, I tried to shift the emphasis of law enforcement away from victimless crimes. We lessened the penalties on the use of marijuana. We removed alcoholism as a crime, and so forth. Victimless crimes, in my opinion, should have a very low priority in terms of enforcing the laws on the books. But as to appointing judges, that would not be the basis on which I'd appoint them. I would choose people who were competent, whose judgment and integrity were sound. I think it would be inappropriate to ask them how they were going to rule on a particular question before I appointed them.

Playboy: What *about* those laws on the books that govern personal behavior? Should they be enforced?

Carter: Almost every state in the Union has laws against adultery and many of them have laws against homosexuality and sodomy. But they're often considered by police officers as not worthy of enforcing to the extent of disturbing consenting adults or breaking into a person's private home.

Playboy: But, of course, that gives the police a lot of leeway to enforce them selectively. Do you think such laws should be on the books at all?

Carter: That's a judgment for the individual states to make. I think the laws are on the books quite often because of their relationship to the Bible. Early in the nation's development, the Judeo-Christian moral standards were accepted as a basis for civil law. But I don't think it hurts to have this kind of standard maintained as a goal. I also think it's an area that's been interpreted by the Supreme Court as one that can rightfully be retained by the individual states.

Playboy: Do you think liberalization of the laws over the past decade by factors as diverse as the pill and *Playboy*—an effect some people would term permissiveness—has been a harmful development?

Carter: Liberalization of some of the laws has been good. You can't legislate morality. We tried to outlaw consumption of alcoholic beverages. We found that violation of the law led to bigger crimes and bred disrespect for the law.

Playboy: We're confused. You say morality can't be legislated, yet you support certain laws because they preserve old moral standards. How do you reconcile the two positions?

Carter: I believe people should honor civil laws. If there is a conflict between God's law and civil law, we should honor God's law. But we should be willing to accept civil punishment. Most of Christ's original followers were killed because of their belief in Christ; they violated the civil law in following God's law. Reinhold Niebuhr, a theologian who has dealt with this problem at length, says that the framework of law is a balancing of forces in a society; the law itself tends to alleviate tensions brought about by these forces. But the laws on the books are not a measure of this balance nearly as much as the degree to which the laws are enforced. So when a law is anachronistic and is carried over from a previous age, it's just not observed.

Playboy: What we're getting at is how much you'd tolerate behavior that your religion considers wrong. For instance, in San Francisco, you said you considered homosexuality a sin. What does that mean in political terms?

Carter: The issue of homosexuality always makes me nervous. It's obviously one of the major issues in San Francisco. I don't have any, you know, personal knowledge about homosexuality, and I guess being a Baptist, that would contribute to a sense of being uneasy.

Playboy: Does it make you uneasy to discuss it simply as a political question?

Carter: No, it's more complicated than that. It's political, it's moral, and it's strange territory for me. At home in Plains, we've had homosexuals in our community, our church. There's never been any sort of discrimination—some embarrassment but no animosity, no harassment. But to inject it into a public discussion on politics and how it conflicts with morality is a new experience for me. I've thought about it a lot, but I don't see how to handle it differently from the way I look on other sexual acts outside marriage.

Playboy: We'd like to ask you a blunt question: Isn't it just these views about what's "sinful" and what's "immoral" that contribute to the feeling that you might get a call from God, or get inspired and push the wrong button? More realistically, wouldn't we expect a puritanical tone to be set in the White House if you were elected?

Carter: Harry Truman was a Baptist. Some people get very abusive about the Baptist faith. If people want to know about it, they can read the New Testament. The main thing is that we don't think we're better than anyone else. We are taught not to judge other people. But as to some of the behavior you've mentioned, I can't change the teachings of Christ. I can't change the teachings of Christ! I believe in them, and a lot of people in this country do as well. Jews believe in the Bible. They have the same commandments.

Playboy: Then you as president, in appointing Supreme Court justices—

Carter: I think we've pursued this conversation long enough—if you have another question. . . . Look, I'll try to express my views. It's not a matter of condemnation, it's not a matter of persecution. I've been a governor for four years. Anybody can come and look at my record. I didn't run around breaking down people's doors to see if they were fornicating. This is something that's ridiculous.

Playboy: We know you didn't, but we're being so persistent because of this matter of self-righteousness, because of the moral certainty of so many of your statements. People wonder if Jimmy Carter ever is unsure. Has he ever been wrong, has he ever had a failure of moral nerve?

Carter: Well, there are a lot of things I could have done differently had I known during my early life what I now know. I would certainly have spoken out more clearly and loudly on the civil rights issue. I would have demanded that our nation never get involved initially in the Vietnam War. I would have told the country in 1972 that Watergate was a much more horrible crime than we thought at the time. It's easy to say in hindsight what you would have done if you had had information you now have.

Playboy: We were asking not so much about hindsight as about being fallible. Aren't there any examples of things you did that weren't absolutely right?

Carter: I don't mind repeating myself. There are a lot of those in my life. Not speaking out for the cessation of the war in Vietnam. The fact that I didn't crusade at a very early stage for civil rights in the South, for the one-man, one-vote ruling. It might be that now I should drop my campaign for president and start a crusade for Black-majority rule in South Africa or Rhodesia. It might be that later on, we'll discover there were opportunities in our lives to do wonderful things and we didn't take advantage of them.

The fact that in 1954 I sat back and required the Warren Court to make this ruling without having crusaded myself—that was obviously a mistake on my part. But these are things you have to judge under the circumstances that prevailed when the decisions were being made. Back then, the Congress, the president, the newspaper editors, the civil libertarians all said that separate-but-equal facilities were adequate. These are opportunities overlooked, or maybe they could be characterized as absence of courage.

Playboy: Since you still seem to be saying you'd have done the right thing if you'd known what you know now, is it realistic to conclude that a person running for the highest office in the land can't admit many mistakes or moments of self-doubt?

Carter: I think that's a human circumstance. But if there are issues I'm avoiding because of a lack of courage, either I don't recognize them or I can't make myself recognize them.

Playboy: You mentioned Vietnam. Do you feel you spoke out at an early enough stage against the war?

Carter: No, I did not. I never spoke out publicly about withdrawing completely from Vietnam until March of 1971.

Playboy: Why?

Carter: It was the first time anybody had asked me about it. I was a farmer before then and wasn't asked about the war until I took office. There was a general feeling in this country that we ought not to be in Vietnam to start with. The American people were tremendously misled about the immediate prospects for victory, about the level of our involvement, about the relative cost in American lives. If I had known in the sixties what I knew in the early seventies, I think I would have spoken out more strongly. I was not in public office. When I took office as governor in 1970, I began to speak out about complete withdrawal. It was late compared with what many others had done, but I think it's accurate to say that the Congress and the people—with the exception of very small numbers of people—shared the belief that we were protecting our democratic allies.

Playboy: Even without holding office, you must have had some feelings about the war. When do you recall first feeling it was wrong?

Carter: There was an accepted feeling by me and everybody else that we ought not to be there, that we should never have gotten involved, we ought to get out.

Playboy: You felt that way all through the sixties?

Carter: Yeah, that's right, and I might hasten to say that it was the same feeling expressed by Senators Russell and Talmadge—very conservative Southern political figures. They thought it was a serious mistake to be in Vietnam.

Playboy: Your son Jack fought in that war. Did you have any qualms about it at the time?

Carter: Well, yes, I had problems about my son fighting in the war. Period. But I never make my sons' decisions for them. Jack went to war feeling it was foolish, a waste of time, much more deeply than I did. He also felt it would have been grossly unfair for him not to go when other, poorer kids had to.

Playboy: You were in favor of allocating funds for the South Vietnamese in 1975 as the war was coming to a close, weren't you?

Carter: That was when we were getting ready to evacuate our troops. The purpose of the money was to get our people out and maintain harmony between us and our Vietnamese allies, who had fought with us for twenty-five years. And I said yes, I would do that. But it was not a permanent thing, not to continue the war but to let us get our troops out in an orderly fashion.

Playboy: How do you respond to the argument that it was the Democrats, not the Republicans, who got us into the Vietnam War?

Carter: I think it started originally, maybe, with Eisenhower, then Kennedy. Johnson and then Nixon. It's not a partisan matter. I think Eisenhower probably first got us in there thinking that since France had failed, our country might slip in there and succeed. Kennedy thought he could escalate involvement by going beyond the mere advisory role. I guess if there was one president who made the most determined effort, conceivably, to end the war by massive force, it was certainly Johnson. And Nixon went into Cambodia and bombed it, and so forth. It's not partisan—it's just a matter that evolved as a habit over several administrations. There was a governmental consciousness to deal in secrecy, to exclude the American people, to mislead them with false statements and sometimes outright lies. Had the American people been told the facts from the beginning by Eisenhower,

Kennedy, McNamara, Johnson, Kissinger, and Nixon, I think there would have been different decisions made in our government.

Playboy: At the Democratic Convention, you praised Johnson as a president who had vastly extended human rights. Were you simply omitting any mention of Vietnam?

Carter: It was obviously the factor that destroyed his political career and damaged his whole life. But as far as what I said at the convention, there hasn't been another president in our history—with the possible exception of Abraham Lincoln—who did so much to advance the cause of human rights.

Playboy: Except for the human rights of the Vietnamese and the Americans who fought there.

Carter: Well, I really believe that Johnson's motives were good. I think he tried to end the war even while the fighting was going on, and he was speaking about massive rehabilitation efforts, financed by our government, to help people. I don't think he ever had any desire for permanent entrenchment of our forces in Vietnam. I think he had a mistaken notion that he was defending democracy and that what he was doing was compatible with the desires of the South Vietnamese.

Playboy: Then what about the administration that ended the war? Don't you have to give credit to Kissinger, the secretary of state of a Republican president, for ending a war that a Democratic president escalated?

Carter: I think the statistics show that more bombs were dropped in Vietnam and Cambodia under Nixon and Kissinger than under Johnson. Both administrations were at fault, but I don't think the end came about as a result of Kissinger's superior diplomacy. It was the result of several factors that built up in an inexorable way: the demonstrated strength of the Viet Cong, the tremendous pressure to withdraw that came from the American people and an aroused Congress. I think Nixon and Kissinger did the proper thing in starting a phased withdrawal, but I don't consider that to be a notable diplomatic achievement by Kissinger. As we've now learned, he promised the Vietnamese things that cannot be delivered—reparations, payments, economic advantages, and so forth. Getting out of Vietnam was very good, but whether Kissinger deserved substantial diplomatic credit for it is something I doubt.

Playboy: You've said you'll pardon men who refused military service because of the Vietnam War but not necessarily those who deserted while they were in the Armed Forces. Is that right?

Carter: That's right. I would not include them. Deserters ought to be handled on a separate-case basis. There's a difference to me. I was in the navy for a long time. Somebody who goes into the military joins a kind of mutual partnership arrangement, you know what I mean? Your life depends on other people, their lives depend on you. So I don't intend to pardon the deserters. As far as the other categories of war resisters go, to me the ones who stayed in this country and let their opposition to the war be known publicly are more heroic than those who went and hid in Sweden. But I'm not capable of judging motives, so I'm just going to declare a blanket pardon.

Playboy: When?

Carter: The first week I'm in office.

Playboy: You've avoided the word "amnesty" and chosen to use the word "pardon," but there doesn't seem to be much difference between the two in the dictionary. Could it be because amnesty is more emotionally charged and pardon a word more people will accept?

Carter: You know I can't deny that. But my reason for distinguishing between the two is that I think that all of those poor, and often Black, young men who went to Vietnam are more worthy of recognition than those who defected, and the word "pardon" includes those who simply avoided the war completely. But I just want to bring the defectors back to this country without punishment and, in doing so, I would like to have the support of the American people. I haven't been able to devise for private or public presentation a better way to do it.

Playboy: Earlier this year, there was a report that as governor of Georgia, you had issued a resolution that seemed to support William Calley after his trial for the Mỹ Lai massacre and that you'd referred to him as a scapegoat. Was that a misreading of your position?

Carter: Yes. There was no reason for me to mislead anybody on the Calley thing. I thought when I first read about him that Calley was a murderer. He was tried in Georgia and found to be a murderer. I said two things: One, that Calley was not typical of our American Servicemen and two, that he was a scapegoat because his superiors should have been tried, too. The resolution I made as governor didn't have anything to do with Calley. The purpose of it, calling for solidarity with our boys in Vietnam, was to distinguish American servicemen fighting an unpopular war. They weren't murderers, but they were equated, unfortunately, with a murderer in people's minds.

Playboy: In preparing for this interview, we spoke with your mother, your son Chip, and your sister Gloria. We asked them what single action would most disappoint them in a Carter presidency. They all replied that it would be if you ever sent troops to intervene in a foreign war. In fact, Miss Lillian said she would picket the White House.

Carter: They share my views completely.

Playboy: What about more limited military action? Would you have handled the *Mayaguez* incident the same way President Ford did?

Carter: Let me assess that in retrospect. It's obvious we didn't have adequate intelligence; we attacked an island when the *Mayaguez* crew was no longer there. There was a desire, I think, on the part of President Ford to extract maximum publicity from our effort, so that about twenty-three minutes after our crew was released, we went ahead and bombed the island airport. I hope I would have been capable of getting adequate intelligence, surrounded the island more quickly, and isolated the crew, so we wouldn't have had to attack the airport after the crew was released. These are some of the differences in the way I would have done it.

Playboy: So it's a matter of degree; you would have intervened militarily, too.

Carter: I would have done everything necessary to keep the crew from being taken to the mainland, yes.

Playboy: Then would you summarize your position on foreign intervention?

Carter: I would never intervene for the purpose of overthrowing a government. If enough were at stake for our national interest, I would use prestige, legitimate diplomatic leverage, trade mechanisms. But it would be the sort of effort that would not be embarrassing to this nation if revealed completely. I don't ever want to do anything as president that would be a contravention of the moral and ethical standards that I would exemplify in my own life as an individual or that would violate the principles or character of the American people.

Playboy: Do you feel it's fair criticism that you seem to be going back to some familiar faces—such as Paul Warnke and Cyrus Vance—for foreign-policy advice? Isn't there a danger of history's repeating itself when you seek out those who were involved in our Vietnam decisions?

Carter: I haven't heard that criticism. If you're raising it, then I respond to the new critic. These people contribute to foreign-affairs journals, they individually explore different concepts of foreign policy. I have fifteen or twenty people who work with me very closely on foreign affairs. Their views are quite divergent. The fact that they may or may not have been involved in foreign-policy decisions in the past is certainly no detriment to their ability to help me now.

Playboy: In some respects, your foreign policy seems similar to that established by Kissinger, Nixon, and Ford. In fact, Kissinger stated that he didn't think your differences were substantial. How, precisely, does your view differ from theirs?

Carter: As I've said in my speeches, I feel the policy of détente has given up too much to the Russians and gotten too little in return. I also feel Kissinger has equated his own popularity with the so-called advantages of détente. As I've traveled and spoken with world leaders—Helmut Schmidt of West Germany, Yitzhak Rabin of Israel, various leaders in Japan—I've discerned a deep concern on their part that the United States has abandoned a long-standing principle: to consult mutually, to share responsibility for problems. This has been a damaging thing. In addition, I believe we should have stronger bilateral relations with developing nations.

Playboy: What do you mean when you say we've given up too much to the Russians?

Carter: One example I've mentioned often is the Helsinki agreement. I never saw any reason we should be involved in the Helsinki meetings at all. We added the stature of our presence and signature to an agreement that, in effect, ratified the take-over of eastern Europe by the Soviet Union. We got very little, if anything, in return. The Russians promised they would honor democratic principles and permit the free movement of their citizens, including those who want to emigrate. The Soviet Union has not lived up to those promises and Mr. Brezhnev was able to celebrate the major achievement of his diplomatic life.

Playboy: Are you charging that Kissinger was too soft on the Russians?

Carter: Kissinger has been in the position of being almost uniquely a spokesman for our nation. I think that is a legitimate role and a proper responsibility of the president himself. Kissinger has had a kind of Lone Ranger, secret foreign-policy attitude, which almost ensures that there cannot be adequate consultation with our allies; there cannot be a long-range commitment to unchanging principles; there cannot be a coherent evolution on foreign policy; there cannot be a bipartisan approach with support and advice from Congress. This is what I would avoid as president and is one of the major defects in the Nixon-Ford foreign policy as expressed by Kissinger.

Playboy: Say, do you always do your own sewing?

[*This portion of the interview also took place aboard a plane. As he answered the interviewer's questions, Carter had been sewing a rip in his jacket with a needle and thread he carried with him.*]

Carter: Uh-huh. [*He bit off the thread with his teeth.*]

Playboy: Anyway, you said earlier that your foreign policy would exemplify your moral and ethical standards. Isn't there as much danger in an overly moralistic policy as in the kind that is too pragmatic?

Carter: I've said I don't think we should intervene militarily, but I see no reason not to express our approval, at least verbally, with those nations that develop democratically. When Kissinger says, as he did recently in a speech, that Brazil is the sort of government that is most compatible with ours—well, that's the kind of thing we want to change. Brazil is not a democratic government; it's a military dictatorship. In many instances, it's highly repressive to political prisoners. Our government should justify the character and moral principles of the American people, and our foreign policy should not short-circuit that for temporary advantage. I think in every instance we've done that it's been counterproductive. When the CIA undertakes covert activities that might be justified if they were peaceful, we always suffer when they're revealed—it always seems as if we're trying to tell other people how to act. When Kissinger and Ford warned Italy she would be excluded from NATO if the Communists assumed power, that was the best way to make sure Communists were elected. The Italian voters resent it. A proper posture for our country in this sort of situation is to show, through demonstration, that our own government works properly, that democracy is advantageous, and let the Italian people make their own decisions.

Playboy: And what if the Communists in Italy had been elected in greater numbers than they were? What if they had actually become a key part of the Italian government?

Carter: I think it would be a mechanism for subversion of the strength of NATO and the cohesiveness that ought to bind European countries together. The proper posture was the one taken by Helmut Schmidt, who said that German aid to Italy would be endangered.

Playboy: Don't you think that constitutes a form of intervention in the democratic processes of another nation?

Carter: No, I don't. I think that when the democratic nations of the world express themselves frankly and forcefully and openly, that's a proper exertion of influence. We did the same thing in Portugal. Instead of going in through surreptitious means and trying to overthrow the government when it looked like the minority Communist Party was going to assume power, the NATO countries as a group made it clear to Portugal what it would lose in the way of friendship, trade opportunities, and so forth. And the Portuguese people, recognizing that possibility, decided that the Communists should not lead their government. Well, that was legitimate exertion of influence, in my opinion. It was done openly and it was a mere statement of fact.

Playboy: You used the word subversion referring to communism. Hasn't the world changed since we used to throw words like that around? Aren't the west European communist parties more independent of Moscow and more willing to respect democracy?

Carter: Yes, the world's changed. In my speeches, I've made it clear that as far as Communist leaders in such countries as Italy, France and Portugal are concerned, I would not want to close the doors of communication, consultation, and friendship to them. That would be an almost automatic forcing of the Communist leaders into the Soviet sphere of influence. I also think we should keep open our opportunities for the east European nations—even those that are completely Communist—to trade with us, understand us, have tourist exchange, and give them an option from complete domination by the Soviet Union.

But again, I don't think you could expect West Germany to lend Poland two billion dollars—which was the figure in the case of Italy—when Poland is part of the Soviet government's satellite and supportive-nation group. So I think the best way to minimize totalitarian influence within the governments of Europe is to make sure the democratic forces perform properly. The major shift toward the Communists in Italy was in the local elections, when the Christian Democrats destroyed their reputation by graft and corruption. If we can make our own government work, if we can avoid future Watergates and avoid the activities of the CIA that have been revealed, if we can minimize joblessness and inflation, this will be a good way to lessen the inclination of people in other countries to turn away from our form of government.

Playboy: What about Chile? Would you agree that that was a case of the United States, through the CIA, intervening improperly?

Carter: Yes. There's no doubt about it. Sure.

Playboy: And you would stop that sort of thing?

Carter: Absolutely. Yes, sir.

Playboy: What about economic sanctions? Do you feel we should have punished the Allende government the way we did?

Carter: That's a complicated question, because we don't know what caused the fall of the Allende government, the murder of perhaps thousands of people, the incarceration of many others. I don't have any facts as to how deeply involved we were, but my impression is that we were involved quite deeply. As I said, I wouldn't have done that if I were president. But as to whether or not we ought to have an option on the terms of our loans, repayment schedules, interest charges, the kinds of materials we sell to them—those are options I would retain depending upon the compatibility of a foreign government with our own.

Playboy: To what do you attribute all those deceptions and secret maneuverings through the years? Why were they allowed to happen?

Carter: It was a matter of people's just saying, "Well, that's politics; we don't have a right to know what our government is doing; secrecy is okay; accepting gifts is okay; excluding the American people is okay." These are the kinds of things I want to change.

Playboy: It sounds as if you're saying Americans accepted indecency and lies in their government all too easily. Doesn't that make your constant campaign theme, invoking the decency and honesty of the American people, somewhat naive and ingenuous?

Carter: I say that the American people are basically decent and honest and want a truthful government. Obviously, I know there are people in this country, out of 214,000,000, who are murderers. There are people, maybe, who don't want a decent government. Maybe there are people who prefer lies to truth. But I don't think it's simplistic to say that our government hasn't measured up to the ethical and moral standards of the people of this country. We've had better governments in the past and I think our people, as I've said many times, are just as strong, courageous and intelligent as they were 200 years ago. I think we still have the same inner strength they had then.

Playboy: Even though a lot of people support that feeling, many others think it makes you sound like an evangelist. And that makes it all the more confusing when they read about your hanging out with people so different from you in lifestyle and beliefs. Your publicized friendship with journalist Hunter Thompson, who makes no secret of his affinity for drugs and other craziness, is a good example.

Carter: Well, in the first place, I'm a human being. I'm not a packaged article that you can put in a little box and say, "Here's a Southern Baptist, an ignorant Georgia peanut farmer who doesn't have the right to enjoy music, who has no flexibility in his mind, who can't understand the sensitivities of an interpersonal relationship. He's gotta be predictable. He's gotta be for Calley and for the war. He's gotta be a liar. He's gotta be a racist." You know, that's the sort of stereotype people tend to assume, and I hope it doesn't apply to me. And I don't see any mystery about having a friendship with Hunter Thompson. I guess it's something that's part of my character and it becomes a curiosity for those who see some mystery about someone of my background being elected president. I'm just a human being like everybody else. I have different interests, different understandings of the world around me, different relationships with different kinds of people. I have a broad range of friends: sometimes very serious, sometimes very formal, sometimes lighthearted, sometimes intense, sometimes casual.

Playboy: So when you find yourself at a rock concert or in some other situation that seems at odds with your rural, religious background, you never feel a sense of estrangement?

Carter: None. No. I feel at home with 'em.

Playboy: How did you get to feel this way without going through culture shock?

Carter: I have three sons, who now range from twenty-three to twenty-nine, and the oldest of them were very influenced by Bob Dylan in their attitudes toward civil rights, criminal justice, and the Vietnam War. This was about the period of time I was entering politics. I've been fairly close to my sons and their taste in music influenced my taste, and I was able to see the impact of Bob Dylan's attitudes on young people. And I was both gratified by and involved emotionally in those changes of attitudes.

Later, when I became governor, I was acquainted with some of the people at Capricorn Records in Macon—Otis Redding and others. It was they who began to meld the white and Black music industries, and that was quite a sociological change for our region. So as I began to travel around Georgia, I made contact a few days every month or two with Capricorn Records, just to stay in touch with people in the state, and got to know all the Allman brothers, Dickey Betts, and others. Later on, I met Charlie Daniels and the Marshall Tucker Band.

Then I decided to run for president. I didn't have any money and didn't have any political base, so I had to depend substantially on the friends I already had. One of my potential sources for fund raising and for recruiting young volunteers was the group of recording stars I already knew. So we began to have concerts and I got to know them even better.

Of course, I've also been close to the country-music folks in Georgia, as well as the Atlanta Symphony Orchestra. The first large contribution I got—$1,000—was from Robert Shaw, the music director of the orchestra. We've been over at the Grand Ole Opry a few times and gotten to know people like Chubby Jackson and Tom T. Hall.

Playboy: There's been a lot of publicity about your relationship with Dylan, whom you quoted in your acceptance speech at the Democratic Convention. How did that come about?

Carter: A number of years ago, my second son, Chip, who was working full-time in our farming business, took a week off during Christmas. He and a couple of his friends drove all the way to New York—just to see Bob Dylan. There had been a heavy snowstorm and the boys had to park several miles from Dylan's home. It was after Dylan was injured, when he was in seclusion. Apparently, Dylan came to the door with two of his kids and shook hands with Chip. By the time Chip got to the nearest phone, a couple of miles away, and called us at home, he was nearly incoherent. Rosalynn couldn't understand what Chip was talking about, so she screamed, "Jimmy, come here quick! Something's happened to Chip!"

We finally deciphered that he had shaken Dylan's hand and was just, you know, very carried away with it. So when I read that Dylan was going on tour again, I wrote him a little personal note and asked him to come visit me at the governor's mansion. I think he checked with Phil Walden of Capricorn Records and Bill Graham to find out what kind of guy is this, and he was assured I didn't want to use him, I was just interested in his music.

The night he came, we had a chance to talk about his music and about changing times and pent-up emotions in young people. He said he didn't have any inclination to change the world, that he wasn't crusading and that his personal feelings were apparently compatible with the yearnings of an entire generation. We also discussed Israel, which he had a strong interest in. But that's my only contact with Bob Dylan, that night.

Playboy: That brings us back to the reason so many people find it hard to get a handle on you: on the one hand, your association with youth culture, civil rights, and other liberal movements; and on the other, your apparent conservatism on many issues. Would you care to put it in a nutshell for us?

Carter: I'll try. On human rights, civil rights, environmental quality, I consider myself to be very liberal. On the management of government, on openness of government, on strengthening individual liberties and local levels of government, I consider myself a conservative. And I don't see that the two attitudes are incompatible.

Playboy: Then let's explore a few more issues. Not everyone is sure, for instance, what you mean by your call for tax reform. Does it mean that the burden will shift to corporations and upper-income groups and away from the middle- and lower-income groups, or are you talking merely about a simplified tax code?

Carter: It would involve both. One change I'm calling for is simplification, and the other involves shifting the income-tax burden away from the lower-income families. But what I'm really talking about is total, comprehensive tax reform for the first time since the income tax was approved back in 1913, I think it was. It's not possible to give you a definitive statement on tax reform any time soon. It's going to take at least a year before we can come up with a new tax structure. But there are some general provisions that would be instituted that aren't there now. The income-tax code, which now comprises 40,000 pages, will be greatly simplified. Income should be taxed only once. We should have a true progressive income tax, so that the higher the income, the higher the percentage of taxation. I see no reason why capital gains should be taxed at half the rate of income from manual labor. I would be committed to a great reduction in tax incentives, loopholes, or whatever you want to call them, which are used as mechanisms to solve transient economic problems; they ought to be on a basis of annual appropriation or a time limit, rather than be built into the tax structure. In any case, these are five or six things that would be dramatic departures from what we presently have, and they should tell you what side of the issue I stand on.

Playboy: Would one of those be increasing taxes for corporations, especially the overseas and domestic profits of multinational corporations?

Carter: No, I don't think so. Obviously, there have been provisions written into the law that favor certain corporations, including those that have overseas investments; I would remove those incentives. Tax laws also benefit those who have the best lobbying efforts, those who have the most influence in Washington, and the larger the corporations are, on the average, the smaller proportion they pay in taxes. Small businesses quite often pay the flat maximum rate, 48 percent, while some larger corporations pay as little as five or six percent. That ought to be changed. But as far as increasing overall corporate taxes above the 50 percent level, I wouldn't favor that. We also have the circumstance of multinational corporations' depending on bribery as a mechanism for determining the outcome of a sale. I think bribery in international affairs ought to be considered a crime and punishable by imprisonment.

Playboy: Would you sympathize with the anticorporate attitude that many voters feel?

Carter: Well, I'm not particularly anticorporate, but I'd say I'm more oriented to consumer protection. One of the things I've established throughout the campaign is the need to break up the sweetheart arrangement between regulatory agencies and the industries they regulate. Another is the need for rigid and enthusiastic enforcement of the antitrust laws.

Playboy: To take another issue, you favor a comprehensive federal health-care system. Why don't you just support the Kennedy-Corman bill, which provides for precisely that?

Carter: As a general philosophy, wherever the private sector can perform a function as effectively and efficiently as the government, I would prefer to keep it within the private sector. So I would like the insurance aspect of the health program to be carried out by employer/employee contribution. There would be contributions from the general fund for those who are indigent. I would also have a very heavy emphasis on preventive health care, since I believe most of the major afflictions that beset people can be prevented or minimized. And I favor the use to a greater degree of nonphysicians, such as nurses, physicians' assistants, and so forth. Some of these things are in conflict with the provisions of the Kennedy-Corman bill.

Playboy: Let us ask you about one last stand: abortion.

Carter: I think abortion is wrong, and I will do everything I can as president to minimize the need for abortions—within the framework of the decision of the Supreme Court, which I can't change. Georgia had a more conservative approach to abortion, which I personally favored, but the Supreme Court ruling suits me all right. I signed a Georgia law as governor that was compatible with the Supreme Court decision.

Playboy: You think it's wrong, but the ruling suits you? What would we tell a woman who said her vote would depend on how you stood on abortion?

Carter: If a woman's major purpose in life is to have unrestricted abortions, then she ought not to vote for me. But she wouldn't have anyone to vote for.

Playboy: There seem to have been relatively few women in important staff positions in your campaign. Is that accurate?

Carter: Women have been in charge of our entire campaign effort in Georgia and in New York State outside New York City. Also in Nebraska. Kansas, a third of the state of Florida and other areas.

Playboy: But whenever we hear about a meeting of top staff members, they almost always seem to be white males. Is that a failing in your organization?

Carter: I don't know about a failing. The three people with whom I consult regularly—in addition to my wife—are white males: Hamilton Jordan, Jody Powell, and Charles Kirbo. But we do have a lot of women involved in the campaign. We are now setting up a policy committee to run a nationwide effort to coordinate Democratic races, and 50 percent of the members of this committee will be women. But Jody has been my press secretary since 1970, and Hamilton and Kirbo were my major advisors in 1966. It's such an extremely stable staff that there's been no turnover at all in the past five or six years. But we've made a lot of progress, I think, in including women, and I think you'll see more.

Playboy: You mention very frequently how much you count on your wife's advice. Isn't there a strain during the campaign, with the two of you separated so much of the time?

Carter: Well, when I was in the Navy, I was at sea most of the time and I'd see her maybe one or two nights a week. Now, when I'm home in Plains, I see her almost every night. And if I'm elected president, I'll see her every night. So there is obviously a time to be together and a time to be separated. If you're apart three or four days and then meet again, it's almost—for me, it's a very exciting reunion. I'll have been away from Rosalynn for a few days and if I see her across an airport lobby, or across a street, I get just as excited as I did when I was, you know, thirty years younger.

We have a very close, very intimate sharing of our lives and we've had a tremendous magnification of our life's purposes in politics. Before 1966, she and I were both very shy. It was almost a painful thing to approach a stranger or make a speech. It's been a mutual change we've gone through, because we both felt it was worthwhile; so no matter what the outcome of the election, the relationship between Rosalynn and me will be very precious.

Playboy: Did you both have the usual share of troubles adjusting to marriage?

Carter: We did at first. We've come to understand each other much better. I was by far the dominant person in the marriage at the beginning, but not anymore. She's just as strong, if not stronger than I am. She's fully equal to me in every way in our relationship, in making business decisions, and she makes most of the decisions about family affairs. And I think it was a struggle for her to achieve this degree of independence and equality in our personal relationship. So, to summarize, years ago we had a lot of quarrels—none serious, particularly—but now we don't.

Playboy: A lot of marriages are foundering these days. Why is yours so successful?

Carter: Well, I really love Rosalynn more now than I did when I married her. And I have loved no other women except her. I had gone out with all kinds of girls, sometimes fairly steadily, but I just never cared about them. Rosalynn had been a friend of my sister's and was three years younger than I, which is a tremendous chasm in the high school years. She was just one of those insignificant little girls around the house. Then, when I was twenty-one and home from the navy on leave, I took her out to a movie. Nothing extraordinary happened, but the next morning I told my mother, "That's the girl I want to marry." It's the best thing that ever happened to me. We also share a religious faith, and the two or three times in our married life when we've had a serious crisis, I think that's what sustained our marriage and helped us overcome our difficulty. Our children, too, have been a factor binding Rosalynn and me together. After the boys, Amy came along late and it's been especially delightful for me, maybe because she's a little girl.

Playboy: This is a tough question to ask, but because it's been such a factor in American political life, we wonder if you've ever discussed with Rosalynn the possibility of being assassinated. And, assuming you have, how do you deal with it in your own mind?

Carter: Well, in the first place, I'm not afraid of death. In the second place, it's the same commitment I made when I volunteered to go into the submarine force. I accepted a certain degree of danger when I made the original decision, then I didn't worry about it anymore. It wasn't something that preyed on my mind; it wasn't something I had to reassess every five minutes. There is a certain element of danger in running for president, borne out by statistics on the number of presidents who have been attacked, but I have to say frankly that it's something I never worry about.

Playboy: Your first answer was that you don't fear death. Why not?

Carter: It's part of my religious belief. I just look at death as not a threat. It's inevitable, and I have an assurance of eternal life. There is no feeling on my part that I *have* to be president, or that I *have* to live, or that I'm immune to danger. It's just that the termination of my physical life is relatively insignificant in my concept of overall existence. I don't say that in a mysterious way; I recognize the possibility of assassination. But I guess everybody recognizes the possibility of other forms of death—automobile accidents, airplane accidents, cancer. I just don't worry.

Playboy: There's been some evidence that Johnson and Nixon both seemed to have gone a bit crazy while they were in the White House. Do you ever wonder if the pressures of the office might make anyone mentally unstable?

Carter: I really don't have the feeling that being in the White House is what caused Nixon's or Johnson's problems. Other presidents have served without developing mental problems—Roosevelt, Truman, Eisenhower, Kennedy, for instance. As far as I've been able to discern, President Ford approaches—or avoids—the duties of the White House with equanimity and self-assurance.

I think the ability to accept oneself and to feel secure and confident, to avoid any degree of paranoia, to face reality, these factors are fairly independent of whether or not one is president. The same factors would be important if someone were chief of police, or a schoolteacher, or a magazine editor. The pressure is greater on a president, obviously, than some of the jobs I've described, but I think the ability to accommodate pressure is a personal thing.

Playboy: We noticed your crack about President Ford's avoiding the duties of the White House. Do you agree with Senator Mondale's assessment, when he said shortly after the nomination that Ford isn't intelligent enough to be a good president?

Carter: Well, if you leave Mondale out of it, I personally think that President Ford is adequately intelligent to be president.

Playboy: And what about your presidency, if you're elected—will you have a dramatic first 1,000 days?

Carter: I would hope that my administration wouldn't be terminated at the end of 1,000 days, as was the case with one administration. I'm beginning to meet with key leaders of Congress to evolve specific legislation to implement the Democratic platform commitment. If I'm elected, there will be no delay in moving aggressively on a broad front to carry out the promises I've made to the American people. I intend to stick to everything I've promised.

Playboy: Thanks for all the time you've given us. Incidentally, do you have any problems with appearing in *Playboy*? Do you think you'll be criticized?

Carter: I don't object to that at all. I don't believe I'll be criticized.

[*At the final session, which took place in the living room of Carter's home in Plains, the allotted time was up. A press aide indicated that there were other appointments for which Carter was already late, and the aide opened the front door while amenities were exchanged. As the interviewer and the* Playboy *editor stood at the door, recording equipment in their arms, a final, seemingly casual question was tossed off. Carter then delivered a long, softly spoken monolog that grew in intensity as he made his final points. One of the journalists signaled to Carter that they were still taping, to which Carter nodded his assent.*]

Playboy: Do you feel you've reassured people with this interview, people who are uneasy about your religious beliefs, who wonder if you're going to make a rigid, unbending president?

Carter: I don't know if you've been to Sunday school here yet; some of the press has attended. I teach there about every three or four weeks. It's getting to be a real problem because we don't have room to put everybody now when I teach. I don't know if we're going to have to issue passes or what. It almost destroys the worship aspect of it. But we had a good class last Sunday. It's a good way to learn what I believe and what the Baptists believe. One thing the Baptists believe in is complete autonomy. I don't accept any domination of my life by the Baptist Church, none. Every Baptist church is individual and autonomous. We don't accept domination of our church from the Southern Baptist Convention. The reason the Baptist Church was formed in this country was because of our belief in absolute and total separation of church and state. These basic tenets make us almost unique. We don't believe in any hierarchy in church. We don't have bishops. Any officers chosen by the church are defined as servants, not bosses. They're supposed to do the dirty work, make sure the church is clean and painted and that sort of thing. So it's a very good, democratic structure. When my sons were small, we went to church and they went, too. But when they got old enough to make their own decisions, they decided when to go and they varied in their devoutness. Amy really looks forward to going to church, because she gets to see all her cousins at Sunday school. I never knew anything except going to church. My wife and I were born and raised in innocent times. The normal thing to do was to go to church. What Christ taught about most was pride, that one person should never think he was any better than anybody else. One of the most vivid stories Christ told in one of his parables was about two people who went into a church. One was an official of the church, a Pharisee, and he said, "Lord, I thank you that I'm not like all those other people. I keep all your commandments, I give a tenth of everything I own. I'm here to give thanks for making me more acceptable in your sight." The other guy was despised by the nation, and he went in, prostrated himself on the floor and said, "Lord, have mercy on me, a sinner. I'm not worthy to lift my eyes to heaven." Christ asked the disciples which of the two had justified his life. The answer was obviously the one who was humble. The thing that's drummed into us all the time is not to be proud, not to be better than anyone else, not to look down on people but to make ourselves acceptable in God's eyes through our own actions and recognize the simple truth that we're saved by grace. It's just a free gift through faith in Christ. This gives us a mechanism by which we can relate permanently to God. I'm not speaking for other people, but it gives me a sense of peace and equanimity and assurance. I try not to commit a deliberate sin. I recognize that I'm going to do it anyhow, because I'm human and I'm tempted. And Christ set some almost impossible standards for us. Christ said, "I tell you that anyone who looks on a woman with lust has in his heart already committed adultery." I've looked on a lot of women with lust. I've committed adultery in my heart many times. This is something that God recognizes I will do—and I have done it—and God forgives me for it. But that doesn't mean that I condemn someone who not only looks on a woman with lust but who leaves his wife and shacks up with somebody out of wedlock.

Christ says, Don't consider yourself better than someone else because one guy screws a whole bunch of women while the other guy is loyal to his wife. The guy who's loyal to his wife ought not to be condescending or proud because of the relative degree of sinfulness. One thing that Paul Tillich said was that religion is a search for the truth about man's existence and his relationship with God and his fellow man; and that once you stop searching and think you've got it made—at that point, you lose your religion. Constant reassessment, searching in one's heart—it gives me a feeling of confidence.

I don't inject these beliefs in my answers to your secular questions.

[*Carter clenched his fist and gestured sharply.*]

But I don't think I would ever take on the same frame of mind that Nixon or Johnson did—lying, cheating, and distorting the truth. Not taking into consideration my hope for my strength of character, I think that my religious beliefs alone would prevent that from happening to me. I have that confidence. I hope it's justified.

Interview with the President

Bill Moyers / 1978

Public Broadcasting Service, November 13, 1978. © The American Presidency Project.

Views on the Presidency

Bill Moyers: Mr. President, a philosopher you have read and quoted, Søren Kierkegaard, once wrote an essay called "For Self-Examination." Confession and examination have a long history in your church, although not usually on television. With your permission, I'd like to ask a few questions for self-examination.

If there is a single dominant criticism by your supporters of the Carter administration, it is that for the first eighteen months there was no single theme, no vision of what it is you want to do. Are you going to try to, in the next two years, mold a Carter vision of the country?

President Jimmy Carter: Well, I think it was also Kierkegaard who said that every man is an exception. And the multiplicity of responsibilities that a president has, the same issues that our nation has to face, I think, causes some lack of a central focus quite often.

We're dealing with the question of a strong national defense, some concern about the good intentions of potential adversaries like the Soviet Union, on the one hand. At the same time we are struggling valiantly to find common ground on which we can assure peace between us and better friendship and a minimization of the distrust.

We, at the same time—we're with SALT, are trying to bring peace to the Mideast, to Cyprus, to Namibia, to Rhodesia, to Nicaragua, exerting a leadership role in our country that the rest of the world sometimes expects. And then, of course, on domestic issues, they are so broad—trying to have a strong farm economy, increase exports, stabilize prices with an anti-inflation program, meet the necessary demands of many interest groups in our nation who are quite benevolent. So, to bring some tightly drawn, simplistic cohesion into this broadly diverse responsibility is almost impossible.

I think in some cases previous presidents have had their thrust identified with a simple slogan only in retrospect. I know that Roosevelt's New Deal was identified well into his term, and when he used the expression in a speech, he had no idea that it would categorize what he'd brought to the country. So, I think that only when an administration is looked at in maybe at least a recently historical perspective can you get a central theme.

We are trying to restore trust in government. We're trying to have enhancement of world peace, focusing on human rights, and at the same time exemplify what I tried to express in the campaign, and since I've been in office, as well, that my party and what I stand for is a proper blending of both compassion and competence.

In the past we've not been able to bridge that gap adequately. I think we've made a step in the right direction, but how to bring one or two phrases or a slick, little slogan to identify an administration in its formative stage or even in its productive stage is almost impossible.

Moyers: If I could put it another way, T. S. Eliot once said that every large, new figure in literature changes our perception of literature. I think the same is probably true of the presidency. It represents something of what the country is all about. You're the most recent representative of that tradition, and I'm wondering if, two years into your administration, you know what it is you'd like to leave.

President: I don't think my goals have changed much since I began thinking about running for president, even four years before I was elected, and in the last two years.

There's no doubt that our nation had been damaged very severely by the Vietnam War and by the Watergate scandals and by the CIA revelations. And I think our people were also beginning to suspect that many key public officials were dishonest, not exactly forthcoming in telling the truth, and that there was no respect for our own country among the vast majority of nations in the rest of the world. There was some doubt about our own allies and friends that we espoused who were personifications of human rights violations.

And I think in all those respects—how people look upon our government, either from the point of view of an American citizen and also foreign leaders and citizens—that we've made good progress toward reaching the goal of restoring that accurate image of a good nation with integrity and purpose, openness, and also with a president who speaks accurately for the people themselves.

One problem has been that in the openness that I've tried to create, there comes with debate on complicated issues an absence of clarity. The simplest decisions that I have to make, as I told the FFA convention in Kansas City last week, are the ones about which I know least, that the more you know about the subject, all the complexities on both sides, the detailed, intricate arguments, the more difficult it is to make a decision. If you don't know much about a subject, you can make a very quick and easy decision.

But I think that we have made good progress in correcting some of the defects that existed in our government, and I feel that history will look with favor now.

Moyers: As you talk, it occurs to me that not since 1960 has a president finished two terms in the White House. Kennedy was elected and assassinated, Johnson was elected and discredited, Nixon was elected and disgraced, Ford was appointed and defeated. Would you like to be the first president to finish two terms since 1960?

President: Well, I haven't decided that yet. I would like to be worthy of that honor, and if I decided to run for reelection in 1980, I intend to win. But I can see why it's difficult for a president to serve two terms. You are the personification of problems, and when you address a problem, even successfully, you become identified with it. And that's what the responsibility of the presidency is.

Moyers: Is that why, Mr. President, this disorder has been growing around the presidency? For almost fifteen years now, there is a sense of almost as if the American people or a substantial representative of the American people have silently withdrawn their support from the presidency, no longer look to it as the symbol of the nation as a whole.

President: I think that's true. But there were some special circumstances that relate to those presidents you mentioned. Kennedy was assassinated. I don't think that was any reflection on the presidency itself. It was just a tragic occurrence that I hope will never be repeated.

Johnson was, I think, looked upon by the country as primarily the one responsible for the continuation of the Vietnam War, and the war was around his neck like an anvil, pulling him down. I think he did the best he could to terminate the war, and I know he suffered personally because of the loss of American lives in Vietnam.

Nixon, of course, his successor, had the special problem with Watergate, and Ford was identified with the pardon of Nixon and didn't have long enough to get himself established, I think, to stay in office.

So, there have been special circumstances, but I don't believe that it is inherent in the office that you would be forced out of office because of some adverse occurrence.

Moyers: You don't agree with one of your predecessors that it's a splen-
did misery?

President: No. I think that was President Nixon who said it was a splen-
did misery.

Moyers: Quoting before him some earlier—it was Adams, I think.

President: Before Watergate, yes.

No, I've not been miserable in the job. I might point out that it's voluntary.
Nobody in my memory has been forced to serve as president. And as a
matter of fact, in spite of the challenges and problems and, sometimes,
disappointments and criticisms, I really enjoy it.

Moyers: What's the hardest part?

President: I think the hardest part is the attempt to correlate sharply
conflicting ideas from worthy people. The easy problems don't arrive on
this desk. You know, the easy problems are solved in the life of an individual
person or within a family or perhaps in a city hall or a county courthouse or,
at the worst, in a state capitol. The ones that can't be solved after all those
intense efforts arrive here in the White House to be solved, and they're
quite difficult ones. And I think the attempt to correlate those conflicting
ideas probably bring about the most serious challenge to a president.

Moyers: You said not long ago, "I feel like my life now is one massive
multiple-choice examination, where things are put in front of me and I have
to make the difficult choice." Can you give me an example of that?

President: Yes. I haven't found anything easy about this job. But I
didn't expect it to be easy when I came here. Well, I mentioned one earlier,
the fact that we have to be very protective of our nation's security and
cover every eventuality if we don't make progress toward peace with the
Soviet Union.

At the same time, we have to explore every possibility to have a peaceful
relationship with the Soviet Union, to alleviate tensions and to find common
grounds on which we can actually build friendships in the future. And these
two are not only extremely complicated, each side of that possibility, but
apparently are in conflict.

US-Soviet Relations

Moyers: What do you think the Soviets are up to, Mr. President? I mean,
do you see them as primarily a defensive power, seeking to solidify their
own position in the world, or do you see them as an aggressive power, seeking to enlarge their position in the world?

President: Well, to be perhaps excessively generous, but not too far off the mark, I think, first of all, they want peace and security for their own people, and they undoubtedly exaggerate any apparent threat to themselves and have to, to be sure that they are able to protect themselves. At the same time, as is the case with us, they would like to expand their influence among other people in the world, believing that their system of government, their philosophy is the best. This means that we have to plan in the future, in the presence of peace between us, to be competitive with them and able to compete both aggressively and successfully.

But I would say that those are their two basic motives, as is the case with us—security for themselves and to have their own influence felt in the rest of the world as much as possible.

Moyers: There is a school of thought which says that their aim is to achieve superiority over us in both conventional and strategic weapons and that we must therefore not settle to be equal with them, but to have superiority over them. These are the hard choices you're talking about. Where do you come out in that debate?

President: They will never be superior to us in national strength nor overall military strength. We are by far the stronger nation economically. Our productivity capacity is superior, and I think always will be.

We've got a vibrant, dynamic social and political system based on freedom, individuality, and a common purpose that's engendered from the desire of our own people, not imposed from above by an autocratic government. I think our absence of desire to control other people around the world gives us a competitive advantage once a new government is established or as they search about for friends. We are better trusted than the Soviet Union. They spend more than twice as much of their gross national product on military matters, but we are still much stronger, and we will always be stronger than they are, at least in our lifetimes.

We are surrounded by friends and allies—Canada in the north, Mexico in the south—two open and accessible oceans on the east and west. The Soviets, when looked at from the perspective of the Kremlin, are faced with almost a billion Chinese, who have a strong animosity and distrust toward the Soviets. Toward the west, in Eastern Europe, their allies and friends can't be depended on nearly so strongly as our own. They have a difficult chance to have access to the oceans in an unrestricted fashion; their climate is not as good as ours; their lands are not as productive.

And so, I think that in any sort of present or future challenge from the Soviet Union, our nation stacks up very well, and I thank God for it.

Moyers: But do you think the number one mentality which you hear many people espouse is a healthy mentality? Is the whole question of being number one one that can ever result in anything but an increasing escalation of tensions and increasing arms expenditures?

President: In nuclear weapons, which is, you know, where our competition with the Soviets is most direct, we've both accepted the concept of rough equivalency; that is, we are just about equal. They have heavier warheads; we have more of them. We have three different systems for delivery of warheads—if we ever need to, and I don't think we ever will have to—that are mutually supportive. We have a much higher developed electronics technology; our surveillance systems are probably as good or better than theirs. Our submarines are quieter than theirs.

We've got an advantage in having a tremendous reservoir of a free enterprise business system that can be innovative and aggressive. We have a much closer correlation between the production of civilian or peaceful goods on the one hand and military on the other.

So, I think that in the case of nuclear weapons, we have an equivalency with them, and they recognize it, and vice versa. Both of us realize that no one can attack the other with impunity. We can absorb, even if we had to, an attack by the Soviets and still destroy their country, and they know it, and vice versa.

So, I think that the horrible threat of surety of mutual destruction will prevent an attack being launched. We don't intend to evolve and neither do the Soviets intend to evolve a capability to destroy the other nation without ourselves being destroyed by nuclear forces.

In the case of land weapons, as I said before, the Soviets have vulnerable borders. They have neighbors whom they can't trust as well as we. And in fact, even in the nuclear field [there are] three other nuclear powers who are potential adversaries in case of a crisis—the Chinese, the British, and the French—in addition to ourselves. We don't have any of those as potential adversaries for us.

But I think for any nation to have a macho attitude, that we're going to be so powerful that we can dominate or destroy the other nation, would be counterproductive. And I don't think that even if we wanted to do that, either we or the Soviets could have that capability.

Iran

Moyers: Let me apply the multiple-choice, difficult options equation to a couple of other contemporary and very live issues. One is Iran. What are the options facing you there?

President: Well, we look on the shah, as you know, as a friend, a loyal ally, and the good relationship that Iran has had and has now with ourselves and with the other democracies in the world, the Western powers as being very constructive and valuable. Also, having a strong and independent Iran in that area is a very stabilizing factor, and we would hate to see it disrupted by violence and the government fall with an unpredictable result.

The shah has been primarily criticized within Iran because he has tried to democratize the country and because he's instituted social reforms in a very rapid fashion. Some of his domestic adversaries either disagree with the way he's done it or think he hasn't moved fast enough or too fast, and deplore his breaking of ancient religious and social customs as Iran has become modern.

Moyers: But he was also criticized, Mr. President, for running a police state—political prisoners—

President: That's exactly right. I think the shah has had that criticism, sometimes perhaps justified—I don't know the details of it. But I think there's no doubt that Iran has made great social progress and has moved toward a freer expression of people. Even in recent months, for instance, the shah has authorized or directed, I guess, the parliament to have all of its deliberations open and televised, something that we don't even do in our country here.

Moyers: You think this is all too late?

President: Well, I hope not. I don't know what will come eventually. I would hope that a coalition government could be formed rapidly. At the present time there's a quasi-military government. The shah has reconfirmed his commitment to have open and democratic elections, maybe within six months or eight months. I hope that would be possible.

Our inclination is for the Iranian people to have a clear expression of their own views and to have a government intact in Iran that accurately expresses a majority view in Iran.

Moyers: But can we do anything to encourage that, or are our hands tied?

President: No, we don't try to interfere in the internal affairs of Iran.

Moyers: We did put the shah in, but you're saying we can't keep him in.

President: I think that's a decision to be made by the people of that country.

Moyers: Does it hurt you sometimes to have to sit back and do nothing when you know there are large stakes in a part of the world beyond your influence?

President: Well, we don't have any inclination to be involved in the internal affairs of another country unless our own security should be directly threatened. And that's a philosophy that I have espoused ever since I've been in the national political realm.

I just think we've learned our lessons the hard way, in Vietnam and in other instances, and we've tried to be loyal to our allies and loyal to our friends, to encourage one person-one vote, majority rule, the democratic processes, the protection of human rights. Obviously, we have not always succeeded in encouraging other people to measure up to our own standards, but I think we've been consistent in our effort.

Moyers: But this is again where some criticism arises in some circles in this country, who say the Soviets have a stake in what happens in Iran and they are free to move clandestinely or any other way that they wish. But if we take the position that you're espousing, we'll sit back and do nothing when we should be in there covertly or clandestinely or overtly, taking a tough stand, saying that we may not like the shah but we need him in power. You're saying that day is over, that we cannot do that.

President: No, we have made it clear through my own public statements and those of Secretary Vance that we support the shah and support the present government, recognizing that we don't have any control over the decisions ultimately made by the Iranian people and the stability of that region. The absence of the success of terrorism, of violence, the anarchy that might come with the complete disruption of their government, is a threat to peace.

We don't have any evidence that the Soviets, for instance, are trying to disrupt the existing government structure in Iran nor that they are a source of violence in Iran. I think they recognize—they have a very long mutual border with Iran, and a stable government there, no matter who its leaders might be, is valuable to them.

This might change. If it becomes obvious that the shah is very vulnerable and that other forces might come into power, the Soviets might change their obvious posture. But that's the observation that we have now.

Egyptian-Israeli Negotiations

Moyers: What about the Middle East, Mr. President?
President: I have put hundreds of hours in both preparation and direct negotiation with the leaders in the Middle East, particularly Egypt and Israel. And Secretary Vance, even to the extent of abandoning some of his other responsibilities in foreign affairs, has tried to bring about a successful conclusion of the peace treaty negotiations. There, again, we don't have any authority

over anyone else. We can't use pressure to make the Israelis and Egyptians come to a peaceful settlement of the disputes that have divided them.

The Camp David framework, which was almost miraculous in its conclusion—it seems more miraculous in retrospect than it did at the time—is a sound basis for peace between Egypt and Israel. There's no doubt that both nations would be highly benefited by peace.

Moyers: But yet the talks seem to be at an impasse as of tonight.

President: The present disagreements, compared to the benefits to be derived, are relatively insignificant. The benefits are so overwhelming, in comparison with the differences, that I hope that the Egyptians and Israelis will move toward peace.

Moyers: What's holding it up tonight?

President: At Camp David it was a framework, it was an outline that had a lot of substance to it, but it required negotiation of details and specifics. And there is no way that you could have a peace treaty with all of the ends tied down and all of the detailed agreements reached, the map drawn, the lines delineated, time schedules agreed, without going far beyond what the Camp David outline required.

And so, both sides have demanded from the others additional assurances far above and beyond what Camp David said specifically. This is inherent in the process. And I think in some cases, in many cases, the two governments have reached agreement fairly well.

Now I don't know what's going to happen. We hope that they will continue to work in reaching agreement, to understand one another, to balance the consequences of failure against the benefits to be derived from the success and be flexible on both sides.

These are ancient arguments, historical distrust not easy to overcome. And the frustrating part about it is that we are involved in the negotiations, but we can't make Israel accept the Egyptians' demands, nor vice versa. We have to try to tone down those demands and use our influence. I don't know what will happen about it. We just pray that agreements will be reached.

Moyers: Are you asking both sides to make further concessions?

President: Oh, yes—every day and night. We ask both sides to please be constructive, to please not freeze your position, to please to continue to negotiate, to please yield on this proposal, to adopt this compromise. These have been and are our efforts on a constant basis.

It would be horrible, I think, if we failed to reach a peaceful agreement between Israel and Egypt—

Moyers: What would happen?

President: Our children, our grandchildren, future generations look back and say these little tiny technicalities, phrases, phrasing of ideas, legal-isms, which at that time seemed to be paramount in the eyes of the Egyptian and the Israeli agreements, have absolutely no historical significance. And that's basically what the problems are.

Moyers: Are you saying that the impasse as of today is because of techni-calities and not major principles?

President: Yes, compared to the principles that have already been resolved and the overall scope of things, the disagreements now, relatively, are insignificant.

Moyers: Egypt wants to tie the present negotiations, I understand, to some future resolution of the Gaza Strip and the West Bank. Israel is resist-ing that. Who's being more stubborn?

President: Well, I wouldn't want to start saying who's being more stub-born. I think there's adequate stubbornness to be allotted to both sides.

Moyers: You mentioned grandchildren, and I heard you say after Camp David that at one critical moment that was resolved because of somebody thinking about grandchildren. Would you tell me about that?

President: It might be a mistake to attach too much importance to it, but during the last few hours of negotiations at Camp David, when it looked like everything was going to break down then, Prime Minister Begin sent me over some photographs of me and him and President Sadat and wanted me to autograph them. And the issue at that time was Jerusalem, which was an almost insurmountable obstacle that we later resolved by not including it at all in the framework. And instead of just putting my signature on it, which President Sadat had done, I sent my secretary, Susan Clough, over and got the names from one of his aides of all his grandchildren.

So, I personally autographed it to his granddaughters and grandsons and signed my name, and I carried it over to him in one of the most tense moments and I handed it to him. And he started to talk to me about the breakdown of the negotiations and he looked down and saw that I had writ-ten all of his grandchildren's names on the individual pictures and signed them, and he started telling me about his favorite grandchild and the char-acteristics of different ones. And he and I had quite an emotional discussion about the benefits to my two grandchildren and to his if we could reach peace. And I think it broke the tension that existed there, that could have been an obstacle to any sort of resolution at that time.

Moyers: What does that say to you about the nature of these problems and their resolution?

President: Well, you know, when you put the problems in the focus of how they affect people, little children, families, the loss of life, the agreements and the need for agreement become paramount. When you put the focus in the bands of international lawyers and get it down to technicalities—is a certain event going to take place in nine months or eight-and-a-half months or ten months; is this going to happen before that; is this demarcation line going to go around this hill or through the hill, on the other side of the hill; can the observation towers be 150 feet high, 200 feet high, 125 feet high—the human dimension of it becomes obviously paramount. But when the negotiators sit around a table and start talking, the human dimension tends to fade away, and you get bogged down in the legalisms and the language and the exact time schedule, when from a historic perspective they have no significance.

Another problem has been—and this has been one of the most serious problems—at Camp David we didn't have daily press briefings, and this was the agreement when we started here in Washington, that neither side would make a direct statement to the press. As you know, this has not been honored at all, and it's created enormous additional and unnecessary problems for us.

Moyers: You mean leaks from both governments are.

President: Not just leaks. I mean, almost every day I see interviews in the national television of at least one of the sides in the dispute.

And also at Camp David I was working directly with the heads of state. Here we work with the negotiators, and the negotiators then refer their decision back to the head of state or the cabinet. The cabinet reverses themselves, reverses the negotiators on a language change or one word, and in effect you get the most radical members of the governments who have a major input into the negotiating process, rather than having the heads of state there one hundred yards away so that they can resolve those issues once and for all.

So, I think the follow-up to Camp David has been much more time-consuming and much more frustrating than it was when the three of us were primarily leading the discussions.

Views on the Presidency

Moyers: I read that the Camp David log showed that you spent twenty-seven-and-a-half with Sadat and twenty-nine hours with Begin, and nine hours alone with Sadat and six hours alone with Begin, with no one else in the room, the way F. D. R. used to do with Churchill.

Do you think that you could resolve most of these large issues we face if you could just get people in a room like this and talk to them? It used to be said Lyndon Johnson could have done much better had he been able to persuade people one on one instead of having to use television and public speeches. Do you think that other problems you face could be resolved if you could meet nose to nose, in a sense, with the adversaries?

President: I couldn't guarantee success, but I think, obviously, the likelihood of success would be better.

Moyers: This goes back to something you said earlier, too, where what you try to do is never seen in the singular way in which you're trying to do it, that you become many things to many people. How do you resolve those contradictions?

President: Well, that's inevitable. The most pressing problem on my hands, on my shoulders, is not to present to the people of the world a simplistic and simple character as a president or as a person.

The agenda for an average day for me is incredibly complex, you know, and I shift from one subject to another—from domestic affairs to foreign affairs, from one country to another, from one issue to another. And there's no way for me to say what I did in this one single day in a few words, so that the complexities are inevitable. The only thing I know to do about it is to try to address each item on its own merits and make a decision that I think at that time is the best for my country and my people.

The advantage of having good advisers is very great, and I do have good advisers. I've been criticized because I studied details of issues too much, but that's my nature. And I think on occasion it pays rich dividends, in that I am able to understand the complexities of an issue when a final decision has to be made and not depend entirely on advisers who don't have the knowledge that I, as president, can have uniquely.

But this is a fond hope, I guess, of every politician, to be universally admired, to have all of your themes clearly defined, to have everything packaged beautifully so it can be examined from all sides without doubt, to have one's character be recognized clearly, and to have universal approbation of the people that you try to represent. All those things are hopeless dreams.

Moyers: Pat Caddell made a speech recently in which he said—Pat Caddell is one of your associates—in which he said that a president can succeed by doing poorly because the people out there don't think he can do well. Do you think that's true?

President: [*Laughing*] I hope I don't have to prove that.

Moyers: You were criticized, I know, talking about details, for keeping the log yourself of who could use the White House tennis courts. Are you still doing that?

President: No—and never have, by the way.

Moyers: Was that a false report?

President: Yes, it was.

Moyers: But seriously, is the job too big? Is the United States government, which is a $500 billion enterprise, now too big to be managed by a single chief executive?

President: No. I wouldn't want to—I say that, recognizing that no one person can do it all. But the structure of the American government is still the best that I can imagine. There's a tremendous sharing—of responsibility between the different branches of the federal government, an adequate sharing of responsibility between myself and governors of states and mayors and county officials at the local level of government, between government and private citizens. These balances have been evolved historically, and I think they've grown to their present state because in each instance when a change occurred, tests were made and the best arrangement triumphed.

But it would be a serious mistake to try to run a government like this with, say, a committee. And I'm thankful that my cabinet can be either hired or fired by me. I consult with my cabinet or listen to them, but I make a decision. I don't have to have a vote and go by the majority vote in my own cabinet. And if you had, say, a three-person president, one perhaps involved with foreign affairs, one with domestic affairs, one managing the bureaucracy itself, I think it would be much worse than what we have now.

I like the constitutional arrangement, where you have an executive with constitutionally limited powers and a voice with which to express the aspirations and hopes of our country accurately, I hope, to the people.

Moyers: Was Camp David the high of your administration so far?

President: Well, I'd say the first twelve-and-a-half days were probably the lower of my administration; the last half day at Camp David was one of the highest. It's hard to say.

Moyers: What's been the lowest moment for you? Were you aware, for example, this summer of the growing doubts about your competency to be president?

President: Well, there was a rash of news reports, cover stories in the weekly magazines, and editorial comments around the nation expressing concerns about my ability to run the government.

I'm not sure they were any more condemnatory nor critical than they were about previous presidents, all the way back to Abraham Lincoln; even before. Each president has been criticized and castigated as incompetent and dastardly, even.

Moyers: Your polls had fallen very sharply this summer as well.

President: Well, they had—not as low as the polls fell for, say, Harry Truman during his own administration, but lower than I liked. But I never had any particular concern about that, because I could see in the evolutionary stage, for instance, in my dealings with Congress, progress being made toward eventual decisions by Congress that showed that the 95th Congress had a very good record of achievement. And I think in the confrontations I had with the Congress, when we disagreed on two or three items, I prevailed because I think I was right and established principles that will be good for the future.

But I've never had any doubt about my own resolution. I recognize my own limitations and faults. I'm not omniscient. I'm certainly not omnipotent. I have limited powers, limited authority, and I try to overcome those inherent defects in the office itself as best I can.

Administration Programs

Moyers: What people were saying in circles where I was listening was that Jimmy Carter accepted an energy bill that was not what he wanted; Jimmy Carter settled for a tax bill that was at odds with his conviction; Jimmy Carter had set aside an aggressive fight for welfare reform; he lost his hospital containment costs; he didn't push on education. In a sense, people were saying that Jimmy Carter, who said he was going to bring competency and efficiency to government, was being routed on every front and settling, compromising for what he had said before he didn't want. And from that came a perception, I think, of a weak president, of a president who is being defeated in one front after another.

President: The final legislative agenda as it was passed, I think, is a great credit to the Congress and shows a good compatibility between them and me and has been a matter of pride for all of us.

The fact that we had very few members of the Congress defeated in the last election, compared to previous off-year elections, is good. We still have more than 60 percent Democrats in the House, about 60 percent in the Senate, I think about 60 percent in the governorships, is an endorsement of what the Democratic Party has done.

But I think I need to be fair in saying that there have been times when I've had to compromise, below what I had asked the Congress to do or had demanded of the Congress. We got about 65 percent of the energy bill that we originally proposed to Congress in ultimate savings in imported oil, about 2.5 million barrels a day savings compared to 4.5, for instance.

I would like to have gotten the entire thing. I'm not out of office yet and will come back to try to get some more in the future.

Moyers: But take the tax bill, Mr. President. During the campaign, you said repeatedly our tax system is a disgrace to the human race. The tax bill you signed was a bill that gave the biggest breaks to the wealthiest taxpayers and the smallest breaks to the smaller taxpayers. Did you sign that bill in conscience?

President: That's not exactly fair, because although the bill fell far short of the reforms that I advocated, the bill does bring substantial tax reductions to all taxpayers. And it's a fairly balanced bill, as far as that goes.

It was necessary that a bill be passed and compared to the version that the House passed or compared to the version that the Senate passed, the compromise that was brought about was superior to either one of those.

Had I vetoed that bill after the Congress sent it to me, we would have had an enormous increase in taxes on the American people as of the first of the year; not only the loss of roughly $20 billion in tax reductions that we've added, but also we would have lost, say, roughly $13 billion in tax reductions that had been passed the previous year.

So, there was a case that was a difficult decision to make. When I met a few days before the Congress adjourned with the leaders of the House and Senate—Al Ullman in the House, Russell Long in the Senate—and said, "This is what I will and will not accept," they complied with my request substantially. And although it was short of what I would have preferred, my vetoing of that bill would have been a very serious mistake.

Moyers: This explanation, this rationalization, which is necessary in this town on a lot of compromises, raises the question about where you think the Democratic Party is going. As you know, Democrats have a tradition of using the government's powers to correct the imbalances and the injustices of the capitalist economy, to innovate, to equalize, to take risks. Republicans are elected generally to manage, to stabilize, to pull in the horns a little bit.

Howard Baker is going around town saying—the minority leader of the Senate—saying that "the Democrats are singing our song, and it's a Republican song." And what a lot of people are saying has been reborn in Washington is a conservative administration with a Democratic president with Republican intuitions. Do you think that's fair? Isn't the Democratic Party coopting the Republican philosophy?

President: No, I don't think so. The Democrats have always been a party of compassion and concern about the people of our country. We've always been eager to extend a helping hand to somebody who hasn't had an adequate chance in life to stand on one's own feet, to make one's own decisions, to control one's own destiny, to have an education if they didn't have one, to have a house to live in, to have better health care, better food, security in one's old age, better highway systems. These are the kinds of things that the Democratic Party has always espoused and has always pursued.

I saw quite early in my administration as governor of Georgia that we had an undeserved reputation as Democrats of not being fiscally responsible and not being competent in management. One of the major thrusts of my own governorship was to reorganize the government, to get control of the bureaucracy, to cut taxes, to budget carefully, and I ran my campaign for president on that platform. And we've had remarkable success since I've been here.

We will have cut the budget deficit more than half compared to what the Republican administration had when they went out of office.

We will have passed civil service reform to get the bureaucracy under control, for a change. We've had $28 to $30 billion in tax reductions. At the same time we've had the largest allocation of increased funds for better education the country's ever seen. We've had help to cities and other local governments that's almost unprecedented. We've sustained a home building rate of over two million a year.

So, we've been able to combine, through tough, competent fiscal management, both the delivery of good services to our people and also tight budgeting, cutting down deficits, cutting taxes. And the combination of those two, in my opinion, is not incompatible. You can't educate a child with inefficiency and waste and corruption. You can't feed a hungry person with inefficiency or waste or corruption. And I think that this is a reputation that the Democrats have now assumed, legitimately so, of competent management, that we did not enjoy in the past.

And I can understand why the Republicans are complaining, because they can no longer allege successfully that the Democrats can't be both compassionate, concerned, and competent.

Moyers: If you were a teenage Black youth in the ghetto, if you were one of those millions of people who are surplus in our economy, who have no positive role in our economy or our society, would you have taken much encouragement from the results last week of that election?

President: Well, that's hard to say, when you analyze the results. The Republicans picked up a few extra seats in the House—I think about a dozen—and a few extra seats in the Senate. That obviously should not bring encouragement to anyone that the Republicans have more seats.

Moyers: I mean the rhetoric that many Democrats use, the rhetoric almost everyone used, in talking about cutting back, retrenching, cutting taxes, all of which would add up to a different kind of approach to government than the traditional Democratic posture.

President: I see what you mean. That's hard to say, because for a single person who's out of a job, the most important thing is to get a job. In the last twenty months or so, we've added almost seven million net new jobs to the American economy. We've cut the unemployment rate about 25 percent.

In the case of agriculture, we've increased farm income, net farm income about 25 percent, and as I say, sustained additional commitments to better education, better housing, and so forth.

Now, however, there's a general feeling among those who are in the very low levels of income and those retired people who have a fixed income, that the most serious threat to our nation is inflation. And I think the Congress candidates and those running for governor as well recognize that controlling inflation had to be given a very high priority.

With that comes a need to have tight budgeting decisions made, a reduction in deficits, and a demonstration to the government and also to the private parts of our economy that we are going to be fiscally responsible.

I think in the long run the alleviation of inflation in a person's life is almost as important as an increase in wages or an increase in prices that one can get for products sold.

So, there is a new emphasis, I think, on the control of inflation, but it doesn't mean that we've abandoned searching for new jobs, nor the better life for the people who live in our country.

Moyers: But it is likely, isn't it, that if you succeed in your inflation fight, some people will be put out of work?

President: I don't believe that's the case. We don't project that to happen. I think there will be an increase in the number of jobs available every year that I'm in office. The rate of increase might slack off and level off some, but I don't think there will be a net loss in the number of jobs in our country.

Moyers: A lot of private economists are forecasting a turndown by 1980. How can you avoid that if you really keep the pressure on interest rates and housing construction and the pressures to stop the growth of inflation? Do you have some new trick in the hat?

President: No. There is no trick, and there again it's a difficult decision that you just have to balance. But whether we can continue to build up enormous deficits by spending money we don't have and benefit the American people, is a serious question. I don't think we can.

I think we've got to have careful budgeting, a more accurate focusing of government services to meet the needs of those who need it most; combined with a restoration of confidence in our government's ability to handle both fiscal, monetary, and administrative affairs. And there are times when those are in conflict. But we now have ten years of inflation that's averaged about 6½ percent, and I think that almost every economist, even those who think we might have a recession next year, agrees that we have got to cut down on the inflation rate.

Views on the Presidency

Moyers: Some of your people this morning were telling me that they sense a new attitude on your part, a new spirit of confidence. And they attribute it to the fact that in your mind you've made some very tough decisions on the inflation front and are going to stick with them. Is that true? Are their perceptions accurate?

President: I don't feel that I'm more confident or more aggressive or more sure of myself than I was before. We've made some difficult decisions, ever since I've been in office. It seems to me, almost daily, difficult decisions have had to be made. But, obviously, the longer I'm in office, the more I'm aware of the needs. I understand the government structure better. I know more of the leaders both within Washington and outside Washington who help to shape our nation's policies and shape its future.

We've now finished the 95th Congress work. I think they passed about six or seven hundred bills which help to clarify my own programs. We're trying to take advantage of what the Congress has decided, and I think I'm certainly more aware of and more sure of the opportunities and limitations of the presidency itself.

Moyers: What have you learned about this town?

President: I like Washington very much. We came here as newcomers.

Moyers: To say the least.

President: To say the least. I didn't know the congressional leaders. I didn't know the news media representatives, except those who followed me in the campaign. Neither did they know me. I had a lot to learn about the bureaucratic structure of the government. I was not privy of course to secrets involving national defense or international relations, and I really spent eighteen months or so not only as a president but also as a student trying to learn what I didn't know before.

There have been no serious disappointments on my part. I told some news people the other night at a supper at the mansion that there were two things that had been unpleasant surprises. One was the inertia of Congress, the length of time it takes to get a complicated piece of legislation through the Congress, and the other was the irresponsibility of the press.

Moyers: Irresponsibility of the press?

President: Yes.

Moyers: What do you mean?

President: Well, quite often news reports have been inaccurate when I think a simple checking of the facts with a telephone call or a personal inquiry could have prevented a serious distortion of the news. And also there's a sense of doubt or even cynicism about the government and about programs or proposals, brought about I'm sure by the Vietnam experience, of the fact that the public was misled during Watergate and perhaps even the CIA, as I mentioned earlier.

But I think that a lot of that was caused by my relative inaccessibility and by the lack of knowledge on my part of the press and vice versa. And in the last few months we've taken steps to make sure that we understand each other better, so that I have an ability and my cabinet members have an ability to present the facts clearer to the American people through the press, and vice versa.

Moyers: Is this the work of your media czar, Mr. Rafshoon? What did he tell you about how to get the message out?

President: Well, it was a common belief that all of us had that we needed to have a clearer access to the public through the press in an undistorted way, a truthful way, not to try to cover up any mistakes we made, and also to have it understood among those who report the news that they can have access to me or to Jody Powell or to Hamilton Jordan or members of the cabinet or others if there is a question that arises approaching a deadline, that they can make a telephone call and say, "Is this or is this not accurate?"

We all recognize the devastating consequences of ever making a misleading statement or telling a falsehood, because our credibility would be damaged. And we've bent over backwards (not) to do that. But I think that we've made some progress in this respect.

And I understand the Congress a lot better now. I know the speed with which legislation can be expected to move through the Congress. I understand the complexities of the committee system, the interrelationships between the House and the Senate.

And also I think we're doing a much better job in letting the press have access to the facts.

Moyers: The hour is past. Should we stop?

President: I think perhaps we'd better, if the hour's over.

Moyers: Well, on behalf of Public Broadcasting, I thank you for your time.

President: Thank you, Bill.

Jimmy Carter Works the World

Vicki Quade / 1990

Human Rights 17.1 (Spring 1990).

Since leaving office in 1980, former President Jimmy Carter has devoted his attention to mediating internal conflicts that have maimed, killed, and dislocated millions of people in a variety of Third World countries.

With his wife, Rosalynn, Carter has made visits to eight nations in Africa, Eastern Europe, and Latin American over the past two years, each trip involving a human rights component.

In the past year, he opened peace talks between Ethiopia's Marxist government and the Eritrean People's Liberation Front, another Marxist group that has been fighting for independence from Ethiopia since 1961.

He also chaired peace talks between Sudan and the rebel Sudan People's Liberation Army, at war for the past six years.

Invited to Panama to monitor its 1989 free elections, Carter declared the results fraudulent after Gen. Manuel Noriega stole the election. He was then invited by Nicaraguan President Daniel Ortega to help monitor its 1990 elections and is credited with negotiating a smooth transfer of power from the ousted Ortega to the newly elected president Violeta Chamorro.

Following the Nicaraguan elections, Carter left for a two-week tour of the Middle East to explore the latest developments in Arab-Israeli peace efforts.

Arriving in Syria, Carter discussed the plight of US and other foreign hostages in Lebanon, raising some hope for their release.

After living in political obscurity during the eight years of the Reagan administration, Jimmy Carter seems to be everywhere. At the age of sixty-five, he is enjoying a resurrection of popularity and political importance.

As the thirty-nineth president of the United States, James Earl Carter was the first president from the Deep South since before the Civil War. He was also the first president to make human rights a legitimate foreign policy concern.

While considered even by critics as a decent and honorable man, he was not seen as a strong president. His tenure in office was marked by wide criticism for the poor state of the US economy and for nearly 20 percent inflation.

Despite his success in clinching the 1979 Israeli-Egypt peace pact, Carter was viewed as weak in handling foreign policy, reacting to the Soviet invasion of Afghanistan by imposing a grain embargo and boycotting the Olympic Games in Moscow.

During his last year in office, he almost single-mindedly devoted his attention to securing the release of the remaining fifty-two American hostages held in Iran, but his failure to obtain their swift release plagued him at the end of his term.

The hostages were finally released on Inauguration Day, as Ronald Reagan was taking his oath of office.

A graduate of the US Naval Academy, Carter had studied nuclear physics before leaving the military to take over the family business, which included its prosperous peanut farms.

Entering politics as a Georgia state senator, he served as the state's governor and ran for the presidency in 1976, using the post-Watergate slogan: "I will never lie to you."

He had placed his peanut warehouse into a blind trust during his four-year term and discovered in 1980 that it was deeply in debt. Forced to sell the warehouse in order to meet the debt, he was left with two family farms totaling 2,000 acres and his own modest home on 170 acres in Plains, Georgia.

A deeply religious man, Carter turned his attention once again to foreign affairs, a gutsy choice considering his reputation in the field, resolving to help Third World countries involved in complex and bitter internal battles. The single-mindedness and relentlessness that served him during the Iran hostage crisis would prove an asset in his new endeavor—the Carter Center.

Operated for years out of Emory University, the center outgrew its headquarters and began collecting the $25 million needed for a new complex. Built with donations from individuals, foundations, and corporations, the new and permanent Carter Center opened its doors in 1986.

The complex of four interconnected buildings on thirty acres north of Atlanta's downtown houses the Carter Center of Emory University, the Jimmy Carter Library and Museum, and the Office of Jimmy Carter.

A modern low-rise design fronted by a Japanese garden and bubbling pond, the complex is also home to Global 2000 Inc., an international aid organization working to eradicate disease and to improve agricultural productivity in Third World countries; the Task Force for Child Survival; and the

Carter-Menil Human Rights Foundation, which awards $10,000 each year to individuals or organizations involved in advancing the cause of human rights.

Stepping inside the center, the first thing one sees is a wall of Andy Warhol depictions of Jimmy Carter. The same photograph of Carter is repeated, each one outlined in thick, black strokes signed by both Warhol and Carter. Other walls feature photos highlighting his career in the White House.

The complex operates on a circular route, all corridors eventually returning to a central desk. Considering how Carter's own political career has come full circle, it seems an appropriate design.

This interview, recorded in Carter's office, was conducted by *Human Rights* Managing Editor Vicki Quade.

Human Rights: Ten years ago, conservatives like Jeane Kirkpatrick criticized your foreign policy record, calling misguided your promotion of human rights standards. Given the astonishing transformations taking place in Eastern Europe, haven't you been proven correct?

Jimmy Carter: Well, Jeane Kirkpatrick has always been wrong about this when she says that certain kinds of human rights violations are acceptable if they come from governments that are compliant with US policy, but if the government is not friendly toward us then they ought not to take up human rights violations.

Even President Reagan abandoned that sort of misguided human rights guideline. And I don't think it's an issue that ought to be fluctuated as presidents come and go.

Human rights should be such a central commitment of our country. All of the administrations, Democratic or Republican, liberal or conservative, should emphasize basic freedom, basic democracy, basic protection from persecution by governments.

People like Jeane Kirkpatrick, thank goodness, have been basically discredited, as it were, by the changes that are taking place because of the constant emphasis on human rights.

HR: Did you foresee these transformations in Eastern Europe?

JC: No, I don't think anybody could have foreseen the changes taking place because of the advent of Mikhail Gorbachev. Nobody could have anticipated that a leader like him would come along.

You have not only the Soviet society open to self-criticism, to self-analysis, to change, but also it's not only granting but supporting the democratization of countries in Eastern Europe.

HR: What is the status of human rights in the world?

JC: There's very slow, very tedious progress in the correction of human rights abuses. I don't think there's any doubt that there's much more accurate and precise identification of human rights crimes. And the fact that they are exposed now more certainly and more quickly reduces the level of suffering.

There are human rights violations inherent within wars, which are quite often overlooked because they are thousand-fold more destructive than the imprisonment of an attorney who is courageous, or the execution of a political prisoner. Here you have hundreds of thousands of people who actually are dying as a result of war.

The stirring of awareness of the destructiveness in war, and the lowering of human and moral standards during war, is going to pay good dividends in the future.

HR: So you see war as a human rights violation?

JC: Yes, I do. Particularly civil wars.

Quite often civil wars are precipitated by an oppressive regime persecuting citizens in their country, and the citizens rise up and fight against them.

Other wars are caused, obviously, by territorial disputes without any demand for independence or by religious schisms. When a war starts, then the normal standards of justice and fairness are just thrown out the window.

Governments use deliberate starvation as a weapon. I'll just give you one example. In 1988, in Sudan 260,000 people died as a result of a civil war. About 85 percent of those were totally innocent people who had no participation in the conflict, but they were robbed of their cattle, they were displaced from their homes, their homes were burned down, and they starved trying to find a place to stay and to retry to find food to eat.

In the process all of the normal legal protections of citizens—freedom of speech, freedom of assembly, freedom of press, freedom of movement—were totally abolished by the regime in Khartoum, as a result of the revolution taking place in the south.

So you have both legal and physical human rights violations precipitated by war.

HR: Even though you say there's been more exposure of human rights violations, has there been more recognition of human rights standards?

JC: Yes, I think so. Not only do you have Amnesty International with increasing effectiveness and increasing membership, you have the Lawyers Committee for Human Rights, physicians organizations.

In addition, you have an improved public awareness through the news media of human rights standards. When they are violated you can detect those violations more clearly than before.

HR: Are governments recognizing those standards?

JC: It depends to a substantial degree on the message coming out of the White House. There's only one voice in the world powerful enough to make every leader stop and say, "What is my record on human rights?" and that is the voice of the US president.

Some presidents send that signal, some don't.

When a person is being persecuted, what they fear most is silence from the White House. What the oppressors want most is silence from the White House.

HR: Has there been too much silence?

JC: I think there's been too much silence. I would like to see the United States raise high and permanently the standards of human rights so that everybody in the world, friend or foe, says to himself: "My personal relationship with the president of the United States, my nation's relationship with the United States, is going to be affected substantially by my human rights record."

HR: Do you think that's going to happen in the near future?

JC: Yes, I think so. Of course, the standards of human rights were in a very bad state in the early part of Reagan's administration.

The first trip Jeane Kirkpatrick made was to meet with the military junta in Argentina that had been responsible for 9,000 disappeared children and adults. The next stop she made was with Pinochet in Chile. The earliest leaders invited to the White House were Marcos from the Philippines, Chun from South Korea.

This was a deliberate signal sent out by the Reagan administration that the so-called Carter human rights era is over.

But later, primarily because of American public opinion, that stand was modified. The present administration is continuing to change the Reagan policy as rapidly and constructively as it can.

The private organizations, watch committees, and other groups involved in human rights are getting renewed vigor and life, and membership. So I feel better, as the time goes on, about our own nation's leadership in the human rights world.

HR: President Reagan's foreign policy seemed to rest on two premises—that Soviet Communism was on the march and had no capacity for reform, and that traditional authoritarian dictatorships might be expected to reform themselves toward democracy. Neither has proven true.

JC: Yes.

HR: Are we watching the age of superpowers drawing to a close?

JC: It's increasingly evident that the superpowers cannot dominate other countries, as we once could do and more recently thought we could do.

If you travel around the world as much as we do, you realize that the most popular and perhaps the most influential person on earth is Mikhail Gorbachev. He is looked upon with great approbation and appreciation in many countries, including our own. What he has done has had a great influence on transforming the political society of the world.

It is not a matter of the Soviet Union now dominating other countries the way they did in the past, but as he permits freedom among those oppressed, he's certainly gaining statute in the rest of the world, if not his own country.

HR: Over the past decade, the US has provided $4.5 billion in aid to El Salvador—more than a million dollars a day. That regime seems impervious to change. If there is no longer a threat from Communism, is there any logic in our continuing to support the bloody regime in El Salvador?

JC: There is still a threat from the [Farabundo Marti National Liberation Front], obviously. But we have not been at all effective in dealing with the death squads in El Salvador, that have been supported indirectly by some in the military. And most of our aid to El Salvador has been to the military, which is much stronger than is the president now or was in the past.

The recent murder of six priests by soldiers in the Army is a crime that should give us a renewed determination, if we ever had a determination, to bring the Salvadoran military into compliance with basic world standards of justice and human rights.

HR: Is that a possibility?

JC: I haven't seen any signs of it yet. One of the test cases will be how rapidly the leadership in El Salvador seeks to arrest, try, convict and punish the soldiers that were guilty of this horrible crime.

It's too early to see, but I don't detect much progress yet.

HR: With Communism undergoing drastic transformations, and the old threat of Communism gone, is there a need to continue weapons spending to keep troops in Europe and military bases in Japan? Can we make massive cuts in military spending?

JC: I don't see why in the next five years we can't reduce military budgets by 50 percent.

And I think we would find a reciprocal agreement to do that in the Soviet Union and perhaps among many of our allies.

This is not at all out of the question and would be very beneficial to everyone.

HR: Even cutting back spending by 10 percent would be an accomplishment. Is our country headed for more recognition of internal human rights, where more money would be spent for education, for social reform?

JC: I think so, but I would hope that a portion of that at least would go to the Third World countries that have suffered so much.

We're talking about a trillion dollars a year, a thousand billion dollars, spent on weapons. About 60 percent of that is spent by the US and the Soviet Union. Another 20 percent by our allies. If we could cut that by half, that would release $500 billion to be used for education, shelter, food.

HR: For raising the standard of living in the world.

JC: Exactly. A large portion of it would obviously be spent in our country, but I hope it would release funds that are not now available to relieve suffering in poverty-stricken areas.

HR: Mikhail Gorbachev informed the regimes within his sphere of influence that they could no longer rely on Soviet military support to enforce their authority. Shouldn't the United States make similar announcements to our Central American allies?

JC: I would hope so. Of course, we're not enforcing those nation's authorities with US troops, but we are doing it to a substantial degree with US funding and by US weapons.

This has obviously been the case with Honduras and El Salvador, though less so in Guatemala. I think the more that those countries are able to democratize, the more we move toward channeling available aid to the civilian leadership instead of the military leadership, the better chance we will have to bring democracy, freedom, prosperity, and peace to those countries.

What we've done in the last ten years is channel enormous sums of money to the military and it means that in a supposedly democratic country the civilian leader is just sitting there serving at the pleasure of, under the domination of the military which is receiving the weapons and the funding from our country.

I would like to see that changed.

HR: Nicaraguan President Daniel Ortega ended his nineteen-month truce with the contras. If you were still president, what would your official response have been?

JC: I spent a good deal of time in Nicaragua to keep the election on schedule and to make sure everyone gets a fair election.

There was a pattern of military attacks and intrusions into Nicaragua by the contras out of Honduras, to which Ortega did respond, I think in a very bumbling and inappropriate fashion by ceasing to observe the truce.

I think that if I were president, which is totally a hypothetical question, I would have done all I could do strengthen the democratic processes leading up to the election, and I would put maximum pressure on the contras to refrain from any military action that might have disrupted the election processes.

We are providing funding for the contras in the form of basic supplies other than weapons and ammunition, and there's no doubt that because of that aid to the contras we have a regular influence on them.

There are still some people in Washington who would like to see the contras retain their viability as a military force, to keep a military threat against the Nicaraguan government, the Sandinista government, and they want to keep this military force intact even after the elections.

I think the contras ought to be constrained. I don't mean disbanded, but I think they ought to be constrained from military action, provided the democratic processes in Nicaragua proceed.

HR: If that would be your official response, what's your unofficial response?

JC: It would be the same. That's why I was in Nicaragua, to try to hold down any sort of disruption that might impede the orderly election processes.

HR: How do you think perestroika will change our foreign policy in the 1990s?

JC: The biggest challenge the United States faces is how to deal with our allies in Western Europe, who will see a reduction in military threats against them.

As there becomes increasing harmony between East and West Europe, the character of NATO will inevitably change. How we deal with this more peaceful environment will be a big challenge to our leadership.

HR: While the media concentrates on changes in Europe, you've been involved in several peace negotiations in Africa. As our foreign policy changes, do you see a need for more US involvement in African affairs?

JC: Yes, I do. And in the entire Third World. What the Carter Center does in peace negotiations is what international organizations and major governments cannot do.

We don't compete with them. We don't interfere with what they do. We deal with civil wars. The United Nations, Organization of American States, the Organization for African Unity, the government of the United States, Great Britain, France, Soviet Union have a policy of not dealing with revolutionaries who are fighting against a recognized government or a government that is a member of the United Nations.

I don't have any such restraint, so I am able to go into a country, meet with its leaders in the capital of that government and also with the revolutionary leaders fighting against that government. And then we try to bring those two into some sort of reconciliation, to have a de facto cease-fire as has been the case in Eritrea since September, and hopefully to find permanent peace in the country.

HR: Why have you agreed to participate in these peace negotiations? In your post–White House years you could spend your time playing golf or getting two million dollars for a speech?

JC: That would be nice. The Carter Center could use two million dollars.

HR: What legacy do you wish to leave?

JC: I'd like the people to remember me one hundred years from now because of peace and human rights, but I've still got to earn that reputation.

Former President Jimmy Carter

Terry Gross / 1993

Fresh Air with Terry Gross, WHYY, January 12, 1993 edition. Reprinted with the permission of WHYY, Inc. *Fresh Air with Terry Gross* is produced by WHYY in Philadelphia and distributed by NPR.

Terry Gross: Next week, Bill Clinton will become the first Democratic president since Jimmy Carter. Earlier today I spoke with Jimmy Carter about his own inauguration, his presidency, and his life since leaving office.

Carter has been praised for redefining the meaning and purpose of the ex-presidency by working tirelessly for human rights, conflict resolution, and fair elections around the world and for improving life in the inner cities at home. First we talked about his new book, *Turning Point*, a memoir about his first political campaign back in 1962.

When he ran for the Georgia State Senate, Carter decided to enter politics shortly after the Supreme Court issued its one-man-one-vote ruling in the case *Baker v. Carr*. This decision threw out the county unit system in the South, that system allotting votes by counties, with little difference between those with large and small populations. [The county unit system] ensured rural white domination of the electoral process by diluting the influence of Black voters and voters in cities. Carter writes he wanted to be part of the new openness and reform in the life of his state and his nation. I asked him why.

Jimmy Carter: Well, I had come home from the navy, having been eleven years a full-time naval officer, submarine officer, started a small business, and had never run for elective office. I was chairman of the Sumpter County School Board in the heat of the integration years. I was concerned about the closing down or the subversion of our public school system. And when and I was disgusted in a way with the slow pace of the civil rights changes in the South.

And then along came the bright halcyon days of the one-man-one-vote ruling, where the Democratic white rural primary was going to be stricken down. I thought it was a new day in Georgia, in the United States, where democracy would prevail and honesty would be there and equality would be ensured. And so I decided I would run for the state senate and the only request I would make, and did finally make, was to be on the education committee. And I entered this little community over in the western part of Georgia and Georgetown, Georgia, and I found shocking fraud, corruption, stuffing ballot boxes, abuse of citizens, that was incredible to me.

Gross: When you say you found blatant voting abuse, what's the worst example of voting abuse that you faced during that first campaign of yours?

Carter: Well, I was ahead in the election going into this little tiny county on the Chattahoochee River just across the river from Alabama. There was a political boss in the county named Joe Hurst. He was chairman of the of the only political organization, the Democratic Committee. He was a state legislator. He was the only state legislator that was authorized by special law to be a full-time state employee. His wife was a welfare director. Georgetown was the only post office in the United States, for instance, where all the welfare checks came to the same post office box, and he and his wife would personally deliver the welfare checks to families that they decided should be on welfare.

One of the prerequisites for getting welfare payment was to vote the way Joe has told them. There's no way to ensure that someone votes the way you tell them unless you know how they vote, so a secret ballot was totally out of the question. Everyone who voted in my election, in that little town, voted on an open table in front of Joe Hurst and one of his henchmen, whose name was Doc Hammond. Joe Hurst watched them vote. They put their ballots in a large whiskey box or pasteboard box with a five-inch hole in the top, and quite often I watched Joe Hurst reach in and pull out the ballots examine them, even change them, when he wanted to and put in ballots of his own. It was literally incredible.

And he was so powerful that he was impervious to criticism. He didn't even care if I saw him cheating. He had control of a district attorney, he had control of a trial judge. He had been indicted eight times on felony charges, convicted four times, but never served a day in jail or paid a dollar in fines. He was so powerful it was unbelievable to me. And so I had that to challenge, and many of the people in that little county were intimidated by Hurst.

The crucial base of his operation was the county unit system. One vote in Georgetown was equal to ninety-nine votes in Atlanta. And this was all legal. It was perfectly legal until the one-man, one-vote ruling came down.

Gross: Well, you say that he was so impervious to criticism, so arrogant, that even when you caught him in the act of fraud, he what would he say? "Well, this is such a simple election that we've decided voting booths aren't necessary."

Carter: So he said, "You know, people don't mind if I know how they vote. Why should we have voting booths?" There were some folding-vote voting booths in the courthouse chamber which he didn't bother to use. He had squeezed people in a little tiny room. So that the only place they could vote was on a counter in the ordinary's office, the probate judge's office, and so he and his assistant could watch each vote counted and cast.

Gross: Well, how do you challenge electoral fraud when the people who you have to take the challenge to are aligned with the same people responsible for the fraud?

Carter: Well, even with his oppression, or inducement of people to vote against me, I would still have won had he not stuffed the ballot box. There were only 333 people who went to the polls that day. There were 421 ballots in the box. When they were counted, 118 of them voted alphabetically. It's down to the last letters in their name, a number of whom were dead, and/or in prison, or living in states in a way off, and they hadn't voted at all.

He was the ultimate appeal in the county in the entire process. In that role that he played this was in accordance with the Georgia law that the final decision in any election held in Quitman County, which was Georgetown (a county seat), was made by the Democratic primary committee that was controlled by Joe Hurst. I finally did win that election but even then, I had to go to the Georgia Senate. And under the Georgia law, the Georgia Senate has a final determination about who will be seated in their body.

Gross: How did you learn—how did you get your fair account?

Carter: Well, I think a lot of publicity had accrued. I couldn't get any publicity at all at first. The local newspapers even in Columbus, Georgia, which is a fairly good-sized town, were kind of in bed with Joe Hurst, or they had seen him do this so long. They thought it was maybe acceptable, or shouldn't have been a newsworthy item, until there was one very heroic reporter from the *Atlanta Journal* named John Pennington, who came down quite skeptical at first about my allegations, and then he on his own initiative went into Quitman County got some old records, and interviewed Joe Hurst and all the other people, and found out that my accusations were true.

And in a few days, this story about my election was a top headline news on the front page of Atlanta newspapers. And so I didn't have to operate in a vacuum anymore. And it was no doubt in anybody's mind who read the newspaper, who listened to the news, that this was a crime of the first degree, in the case of elections.

Gross: You know what I found really interesting? Your opponent in that very first election of yours back in 1962, your opponent Homer Moore, ended up supporting you in your presidential campaign. What happened in those intervening years so he became an ally?

Carter: He was a good guy, and I don't think he had any knowledge about the ballot-box stuffing. This was done by in one of the seven counties by this man, Joe Hurst. Homer was a warehouseman like I was; he was in the peanut business or fertilizer business, and I had known him for a good while. And so he and I stayed at fairly good terms, even during all the court tests—and both of us wanted to win, of course. Later, after I had been governor, and when I ran for president, Homer Moore, and his campaign chairman, whose name was Sam Singer, both went to foreign states, including New Hampshire, and campaigned for me. So you know, we wound up to be, and continue to be, friends.

And so Joe Hurst eventually went to prison for vote fraud and also for dealing in illegal liquor. And when I finally got to the Georgia State Senate, one of the things that I wanted to do, although I'm not a lawyer, was to revise the Georgia election code to correct some of the patent mistakes that had been deliberately maintained over decades or generations in Georgia to permit this kind of thing. And as we were debating the new election code, one of the interesting amendments that was put forward by a state senator from the town of Enigma, Georgia, interesting name, was that no one in Georgia could vote in a primary election or a general election who had been dead more than three years.

Gross: [*Laughter*] Interesting cutoff point!

Carter: [*Laughter*] Yeah, there was a very interesting debate about it, too! People maintained that even though say a husband died, there was a certain period of time after his death when the wife and children could accurately cast his vote the way he would have voted if he had lived. And so how long after somebody's death do circumstances change so much that you can't really figure out how they would have voted?

So as a result of all that, all the Georgia election code has been revised. And there are honest elections in Georgia and, as I said, the one-man, one-vote rule not only applied to Georgia, but to thirty-one other states. One of the interesting things is that in states like Minnesota or Wisconsin, the early immigrants who came to our country, say from Norway or Sweden or Germany, wherever they carefully embedded in their state constitutions, the preeminence of rural communities, so as Milwaukee and Madison, Wisconsin, so forth, built up in size, they didn't have equal votes for their citizens.

As did a small county where they were the votes were counted by counties and not and not by all people.

[. . .]

Gross: How did this affect your view of the American political system? Here you are, you know, a young man, you're running for office for the first time, it's incredibly corrupt. So you decided to stay, and you know, try to do what you could to change to change that system, and so on and so on. But still, I mean, your first encounter with it was a pretty rotten one. Did that predispose you to thinking that there was going to be corruption and that you always had to look for corruption every step of the way?

Carter: I was just totally shocked. You know, I was so naive. I'd never had been involved in politics before. I couldn't believe that something like this could happen in our great nation that was based on freedom and honesty and justice and equality. I couldn't believe it. And had I lost that election, which was seen to be almost certain for a time, I would never have run for office again, probably. Later, though, I saw that that was persistence and tenacity and through marshalling of the of the strong will of people who wanted to have honesty in their communities, that you could prevail.

Also, this was a turning point, not only in my own life, but in the civil rights movement. It was the one-man, one-vote ruling, I think more than any other single action of a Supreme Court or the Congress combined, that really finally brought an end to legal segregation of the races. And out of that, obviously, came my interest in human rights and civil rights.

And now the Carter Center has as one of its major tasks, the holding of elections around the world. We've held election to a number of countries in this hemisphere and in Africa, for instance, and I've never seen any election that was nearly so fraudulent or filled with corruption or dishonesty or cheating as the one in Georgetown, Georgia, when I ran.

Gross: To say that's really saying a lot. [*Both laugh*] You've been around the world watching corrupt elections. What about other elections? How about when you were running for governor or for president? Did you see things around you that were perhaps not as overt, not as blatant as what you saw in the state senate, but were still pretty disturbing or pretty corrupt?

Carter: Well, I hate to say this in a way. But in this last election, and in our country in 1992, we invited some Latin American representatives to come and witness the way we conduct American elections. They were shocked at the unfairness of the American electoral system. We assume as Americans that our election is okay. The things that go on in the United States in an election we would not permit under any circumstances. To be perpetrated on the people in Panama or Nicaragua or the Dominican Republic or Guyana or Sheringham or Zambia.

Gross: What are you thinking of?

Carter: Well, one thing is you can't run for office in this country for president unless you're rich. You know, in most countries in Europe and in the rest of those countries, they don't charge people to present their point of view to the public if they want to be the leader of the nation. Those are free and when I go into, say, Nicaragua to try to end the cultural war by holding an election, I insist that the ruling party—then it was the Sandinistas—have to provide equal access to television and radio for their opponents. And the same way in Zambia last year or in Guyana last October, and in other countries. Whereas in this country, you know, unless you were Ross Perot and could spend $50 million out of your hip pocket, you cannot become a viable candidate for president. Unless you've got millions of dollars to buy your right to let the American voters know how you feel on the major issues. We don't look upon that as a defect in our system, but it's something that would not be acceptable at all in any other country that about which I know.

Gross: What else strikes you as being really corrupt in the American campaign system?

Carter: I don't say it's corrupt, it's just a fact that we take for granted that wealth, or the acquisition of millions of dollars, is a prerequisite to any successful campaign. And I think this has corrupted the Congress in particular. You know that there are legal bribes that greatly influence the decision of Congress on almost any controversial issue. It's a kind of thing, for instance, that Bill Clinton's gonna face on health care reform. He's going to have people that own hospitals, and he's gonna have medical doctors and others that are making enormous profits on providing health care, who are going to pay Congress members through PAC contributions and speaking engagements with a very high fee, and so forth, to vote against basic health reform. And this happens in almost every controversial issue that presents itself to the Congress. It's one of the most disturbing things in our government, and it's rapidly increasing as a problem. It's much worse now than twelve years ago when I left the White House.

[...]

Gross: Before we go any further, I'm going to ask you for a little lesson and etiquette. Do I call you President Carter, Mr. President, our former president Jimmy Carter—what is the appropriate etiquette when you're talking to a former president of the United States?

Carter: One of the nice things about our country is you can call me anything you want to—[*laughter*] Jimmy suits me okay. There is a custom in our nation that if you have been a governor or an ambassador or a judge or president, then you can still retain the title. So if you want to call me President, you can. If you want to call me Jimmy, that's fine.

You know, when I go through Georgia, small towns and somebody is an old friend of mine, I know it immediately when they say, "Hi Governor." [*Both laugh*] Whatever the most intimate relationship is. And the little kids around Plains, when I ride a bicycle or jog by them, if they are very devout or their families go to church every Sunday, they call me "Brother Jimmy." "Hello, Brother Jimmy." And a lot just call me "Hello, Jimmy Carter," but it doesn't matter to me. I never was much dependent on the pomp and ceremony of the White House, even when I was there. And so "Jimmy" seems to be fine.

Gross: Now let me ask you. You've been devoting your postpresidential career to monitoring elections around the world, conflict negotiation around the world, human rights around the world. You also have a project in Atlanta to help empower the homeless and the poor. When you left office, what did you see ahead? What did you think you would do?

Carter: I didn't know. You know, I didn't. And I didn't anticipate being retired four years early! Fairly quickly. I decided to teach and I've been a so-called distinguished professor at Emory University, and now this is my eleventh year and I've enjoyed that professorship. I make most of my income on my books; all of them have been very good sellers.

But when I left the White House, I didn't really know what I had to do except to build a presidential library, which was almost an impossible task for a defeated Democrat who didn't intend to run for office anymore. And I wanted to write a presidential memoir called *Keeping Faith*, which I did, because I was deeply in debt. And the proceeds from selling off all my business, and from the writing of that first book, let me pay off my debt. So the evolution of the Carter Center and the different things in which I've been now involved along with Rosalynn, have been really of developments that we did not anticipate when we left Washington.

Gross: You say that you were in debt. That was important, I believe because your peanut factory was kept in a blind trust during your years in the White House. And when you came out of the White House, it was over a million dollars in the red.

Carter: That's right.

Gross: So were you very depressed that first year? You'd lost the election, you were in debt.

Carter: I wouldn't say the first year. Rosalynn was so much more disturbed by the political defeat. And then I was. Then I was strengthened, really, because I had to give us some good reasons why we had a future of hope and gratification. So I had to think of all the good ideas to overcome Rosalynn's despair. So we worked through that. Okay, I think I was always more optimistic than she was.

Gross: Was there a moment of revelation when it started to occur to you the role that you could take in this nation and in the world as a past president of the United States?

Carter: Yeah, in a way that I didn't anticipate or understand at all then the tremendous crying out around the world for someone that has been president of the United States to help with issues.

Let me just give you one quick example. The Carter Center, now we monitor all the conflicts in the world. We do this every day. There are more than a few—more than thirty major wars on Earth. Almost all of them are civil wars, with horrible devastation. Somalia is just a highly publicized one. They're just as bad in Sudan or Mozambique, and other places.

The problem is that those civil wars cannot be addressed, except on the very rare occasions, by the United Nations, or the US government. It's totally inappropriate for any representative of the UN to communicate with a revolutionary group that's trying to overthrow or change a government that's a member of the UN. So most of these civil wars go unaddressed, or even unrecognized by the American or industrialized world.

And so we go into those areas. I don't have any restraint on me. Because I have been president I'm famous enough and welcome enough to go to an African nation to meet with the ruling leaders, for instance, and also to meet with the revolutionaries and see if they are tired of war or convinced they cannot win on the battlefield. Would they agree to let us mediate and try to bring about a ceasefire at least long enough to orchestrate an election? They may not be willing to sit down in the same room, or to acknowledge one another through a direct negotiation. But as you may know, I'm sure you do, the science of politics is self-delusion. Everyone who is running for office—for mayor or for president, whatever—believes that if the election is honest, and if the people know me, and all these other jokers running against me, surely I will win. So if we can convince both sides, or let them convince themselves, that they can win if the election is honest, and that I can help guarantee that election will be honest, they see a way to become president of that nation without continuing the war on the battlefield. So that is a kind of thing that I see very clearly now, which I did not understand at all. Even when I was president.

[. . .]

Gross: When Bill Clinton is inaugurated next week. There will be five people able to remember the day they became president of the United States. One of them is my guest. Jimmy Carter is back for the second part of our interview. The occasion is not just the inauguration. It's also the publication of his new memoir, *Turning Point*, about his first political campaign. I asked Carter about the high points and low points of his inauguration day.

Carter: Well, I don't remember any low points that day. The happy one obviously was assuming the role of president the greatest nation on Earth, and trying to keep a secret. We had planned a few days ahead of time to get out of the limousine for the first time in history and walk down Pennsylvania Avenue, as just one of a people, and that secret was kept—one of the few secrets, by the way, that we kept while I was president.

And it was a glorious reception; the weather was cold. Now remember that my mother always knew how to take the starch out of people's sails and bring people back down to earth. I was very full of myself and when we left the reviewing stand and started walking to the to the White House, for the first time really, the news media gathered around us and my press secretary Judy Polish said don't anybody talk to the news media. Everybody wants to have an interview and I comply with Judy's request. But typically, my mother said, "Jody [Powell], you can go to hell. I'll talk to whom I choose." And TV folks and everybody got around and they said, "Miss Lillian, aren't you proud of your son?" And I waited with great pleasure to hear my mother's response. And Mama said, "Which one?" [*Both laugh*] So she took the wind out of my sails. That's one of the things I remember about Inauguration Day. But it was a glorious day for us, you know, to move into the historic White House mansion and to take on the duties of the president. I just don't have any negative memories of that day at all.

Gross: What was the most disorienting part of your first day and night in the White House?

Carter: Well, we didn't know how to you know how to deal with the solitude. We were overawed to know that a certain little writing table was actually made by Thomas Jefferson, that he carried around on his horse and wrote, you know, maybe parts of the Declaration of Independence when he was a young person on it, and that this bedroom was used by Abraham Lincoln as an office. You know, the aura of the White House and the humility that you feel occupying the same quarters as those great men was overwhelming.

Also, what do you do the next day? You know, I still—I had pretty well gotten my cabinet firmed up quite early, after the election, and what do you do the next day? To deal with a multitude of issues? I had a very fun agenda. I couldn't get much support, originally from the Congress, although finally my batting average was about the same as Lyndon Johnson's or John Kennedy's. What do you do when you get in the Oval Office? I'd hardly knew where it was. I had visited it once before President Ford invited me in to see the Oval Office after I had won the election. I have to say, though, as a bottom line, and I was quite confident off my sails, I wasn't plagued with trepidation that I was inadequate for the job. That may be presumptuous, but anybody who decides I want to be president of this great country has to be somewhat presumptuous. So I wasn't plagued with an inferiority complex. I felt that no matter what came up, that I could handle it, as well as anyone.

Gross: What about during the hostage crisis? Was there ever a point where you wish that you weren't president? Did you wish that you didn't have this terrible burden on your shoulders?

Carter: Well, you know, about two o'clock in the morning, in April when we tried the rescue operation, and we couldn't succeed, that was the perhaps the high point of despair in my presidency, and I knew that I had to get up early the next morning, about six o'clock and prepare to go on all the morning talk shows, and explain to the American people that the rescue operation had failed. That was a very dismal point.

Also, we knew that an accident had occurred and at one of the helicopters had flown into an airplane, and at eight people had died. And I had to notify those families during that night that their loved ones had perished in our secret operation. There's no way that anything else that happened during the four years could equal that as a time of discouragement and despair.

Gross: Yeah. [*Pause*] You've told us a little bit about what your inauguration day was like. Let's skip ahead to the inauguration of your successor, Ronald Reagan. What were you feeling that day? As you realize that the hostages were going to be released on his watch, not on yours?

Carter: Well, I didn't realize that. I had not been to bed for three days and had negotiated in the most meticulous detail the release of the hostages. Everything was all agreed and the hostages were in the airplane ready to take off at ten o'clock that morning, Washington time. So we were just waiting to get word that they had cleared Iranian airspace. And when I went to the reviewing stand, when I relinquished the presidency to Reagan, and he made his inaugural speech, before I left the reviewing stand, I was informed that the plane had indeed taken off and the hostages were all safe and free. I have to say that I didn't even think about the fact that it happened a few minutes after midnight and after noon time, I just knew that they were free. And that was one of the most glorious, and happy moments of my entire life.

Gross: Even though wasn't on your watch?

Carter: Well, to me, I didn't even think about it. But obviously that became the major story among the news media, that it happened about twenty minutes after I was no longer president. To me that was insignificant, but it has still prevailed. Even your question indicates that it was a historically important fact that it happened a few minutes after I left the White House as a president rather than while I was still in office. So I didn't even consider that as a major factor. Then it was the news media. I think that made that a major factor.

Gross: One of the reasons why that's historically important is that now there are allegations that the Reagan-Bush team negotiated with the Iranians to hold off release of the hostages until after the election. Do you think that there was a so-called October surprise? Would you like to see any further investigation into it?

Carter: I don't really know. I've talked to Gary Sick, who wrote the book and he did most of the investigation. He's a very fun scholar and an honest man and he has done meticulous research. Gary Sick is convinced that there was some kind of an agreement made with the Iranians, that hostages would be delayed in release and that enormous supplies of weapons would be made available to the Iranians if I was not any longer the president. I don't know if those allegations are true. I've never tried to find out.

I've opened up my presidential library to any researchers who want to come and look at all the past records, but most of the evidence would not be in my files. It would be in the files of President Reagan and his campaign managers. I would doubt, and I've always doubted, that President Reagan knew anything about that kind of arrangement. It may be that that Bill Casey, who later became CIA director, and who was President Reagan's campaign manager, did become involved in some negotiations with the Iranians—evidence seems to indicate that—but as I said, I've never asked for nor do I now ask for any sort of further investigation.

[. . .]

Gross: It seems to me your reputation has changed a lot since leaving the White House. A lot of people thought you were an ineffective president when you left the White House, but now your reputation, I think has really risen. People have reconsidered your presidency. Those four years are held in higher esteem, and certainly your work since the president since you left the White House. What does it mean to you to have undergone that kind of reevaluation and come out kind of on the winning end?

Carter: I like it. It's gratifying to see to say the popularity go up and re-assessment of my presidency be made in a favorable fashion. Part of it is kind of inevitable. With the passage of history, people can look back and say now I understand why this decision was made or what the design was intended to accomplish. Or as I understand, in context, that this was benefi-cial. I didn't see at the time the sacrifice that was requested was justified. So I think that that's part of it. And the same thing has happened with Eisen-hower. The same thing has happened with Harry Truman, and with others, so that's part of it. Another one is that the things that I've done since I left the White House have also been favorably reported.

Gross: Let me ask you about one controversy you were involved with in your post-presidential years. And that's the BCCI. Some of your groups were funded by the BCCI. What was your reaction when the discovery of the BCCI as kind of corruption and money laundering and so on was re-vealed, and how did that revelation affect your groups, your funding, your relationship with the head of the BCCI?

Carter: Well, I was filled with amazement. I had no idea that BCCI had that kind of character. We had seen in some of the late news reports that a particular BCCI office or bank, I think in Panama, had been accused of laundering money. And then some of the officials had been indicted and convicted. I never dreamed even then, that there was any sort of worldwide, or allegation of, of criminality when we gave up the BCCI financial support for some of the health programs—particularly, almost exclusively, health programs in Africa and in Pakistan. We just had to go out and raise money from other sources.

Gross: You say you knew nothing about the BCCI's money laundering—

Carter: No.

Gross: —loaning money to drug dealers, and so on. Did you feel betrayed when you found out?

Carter: Well, you have to remember that BCCI was a special operation that was heavily used, I understand later, by the CIA, and others. It had branch banking operations in seventy-two different countries. Its main headquarters was in London, or it was incorporated, I think, in Switzerland, and it was pretty much free of the kind of banking regulations that ordi-narily exist in the world. I don't know if the regulations were any worse for BCCI. They were for the American Savings and Loan institutions.

But anyway, it was a freewheeling sort of banking operation with which I was never involved. I didn't have anything to do with banking operations. But if a leader of a nation, you know, had $10 million that he had stolen from the government, his own government and he wanted to deposit it in a BCCI bank, say in Peru or in some other country, I'm sure they accepted the money. And if they wanted that money transferred to a Swiss bank, I'm sure they did it. Whether American banks do these kinds of things. I don't know. I'm not a bank. I don't know much about their banking business. But once the revelations started, other allegations have began.

It was like a waterfall and you know, it just has worn on, but we did use some contributions from the bank owners to carry out health programs. I'm sorry that BCCI was guilty of crimes. We didn't know anything about it. And we obviously stopped getting any sort of BCCI money as soon as we were familiar with it.

Gross: One more quick question. Looking ahead to next week. What will you be doing on Inauguration Day?

Carter: I'll be going up to Washington the night before Inauguration. I'll be at the Inauguration or when Bill Clinton becomes president. I'll meet my first Democratic president. I've never met one in my life. [*Both laugh*]

And then shortly after that, I'll be leaving Washington. I haven't asked anyone yet where I'll be. I presume as a former president, the only Democratic president that survived, I'll probably be on the platform, but I don't even know that yet.

Gross: Will you be wishing that it was you being sworn in? Will you be glad that you get to leave afterwards?

Carter: I'm glad I get to leave afterwards! [*Both laugh*]

You know, I was asked not too long ago: what's his biggest surprise going to be? The biggest surprise will be if he anticipates setting priorities on issues and saying okay, I'll deal with this the first week or two. And then in March I'll turn to this, and next summer to that, and the second term I'll postpone this. He's gonna be sadly disillusioned because you know, what do you put off? The survival of Yeltsin as a leader of Russia, or Bosnia, or Somalia, or the Haitian refugees wanting to pour into our country, or trading with China, or the or the North American Free Trade Agreement with Mexico, or the erupting war in Liberia? You don't have any way to control the priorities of crises that come before you.

And also, it may be that the greatest crisis of his administration is not at all to be anticipated now. I never dreamed, for instance, that there was going to be a revolution in Iran and the Shah would be overthrown, which was a turning point, you might say, in my own administration.

So I think that's the main thing he's gonna have to be concerned about, but he's a competent, intelligent young man. He's got twelve years of experience as a governor. He's had the ordeal of campaigning throughout this country for a long period of time. He's learned a lot about this nation in the process. He has a goodwill with the American people. He has the ability to reach out and have harmony and cooperation, teamwork for the first time in a number of years in Washington, and I have confidence that he'll be successful as president.

Gross: I want to thank you very much for talking with us.

Carter: Well, I've enjoyed it. Thank you very much.

Unorthodox Approach: Conflict Resolution in a Changing World

Shirin Sinnar / 1996

Harvard International Review 18.3 (Summer 1996).

Jimmy Carter, president of the United States from 1977 to 1981, has earned almost as much recognition for his accomplishments since leaving the White House as for his legacy as president. In 1982, Carter established the Carter Center in Atlanta, Georgia, to advance international health, conflict mediation, and human rights. In the past several years, Carter has made several high-profile visits to crisis areas to assist in mediation. In 1994 his negotiations with North Korean leader Kim Il-sung resulted in the resumption of US-North Korean discussions on nuclear proliferation. Later that year, his visit to Haiti with other US officials peacefully restored President Aristide to power and forestalled a US invasion of the island. In the past two years he has also traveled to Bosnia, the Sudan, the Palestinian Territories, and central Africa to assist in mediation or humanitarian projects.

Features Editor Shirin Sinnar spoke to President Carter in April about his projects and perspective on current international issues.

Harvard International Review: For the past decade you have been a strong advocate of third-party mediation, and the Carter Center has spearheaded that approach to conflict resolution. What special characteristics of non-governmental organizations (NGOs) and other third parties enable them to resolve conflicts with more success than other groups like the United Nations or the US government?

Jimmy Carter: The primary reason for our success comes from the fact that almost all the wars now are civil wars. The United Nations was designed back in 1945 to deal with international conflicts like a third world war. With countries facing internal war, quite often the ruling party does not want to recognize the legitimacy of revolutionary groups that are trying to overthrow or change the government, so this makes it totally improper for any UN official or representative of, say, the US ambassador's office, to communicate with revolutionaries because these official bodies are credited by the ruling party. We do not have any restraint placed on us, and we have very free access to opposition leaders. In addition to that, we build up confidence with the leaders, even those in the so-called "unsavory" regimes, so that we can be trusted. Because we have been previously involved in immunizing children and eradicating Guinea worms and controlling river blindness and teaching small farmers how to grow more food grain, they have confidence in our sincerity that lets them turn to us when they do decide to mediate. So I think it is the unofficial nature of our status that makes it possible for us to provide some communication between groups.

Our prime successes at the Carter Center are with people whom the US government in Washington would not contact. The US government would not permit anyone to talk with Kim Il Sung, although he was very eager to resolve differences between his country and the rest of the world. And for three years he asked the Carter Center to come over there so that he could have at least someone in the rest of the world with whom he could communicate. I had a hard time getting permission from Washington to do so. The same condition applied in Haiti; although President Aristide and Raoul Cédras and acting president Émile Jonassaint all wanted the Carter Center to intercede, we could not get permission from the US government to go until the last minute when war was imminent. In December 1994, no one was willing to talk to the Bosnian Serbs except us, and I finally got permission from President Clinton to let the Serbs send a delegation down here to my home in Plains, Georgia. I set down some strict prerequisites that the Serbs needed to fulfill before I went to Bosnia-Herzegovina, and, once I was there, I shuttled back and forth between Pale and Sarajevo to assist with mediation.

HIR: You raised the issue of the State Department originally refusing to grant permission for you to visit these countries. How would you characterize your current relationship with the State Department?

JC: The relationship is cool at best. I had a very good relationship with Secretary of State Jim Baker when he was there; the State Department was quite cooperative. But since he left, the permission that we have received to go to Haiti and North Korea and Bosnia has come directly from the White House and in effect has been quite upsetting to the people in the State Department.

I had a semi-official status when we went to Haiti, which was not my usual role. But I emphasized that I was going as a representative of the

Carter Center and not of the US government, and the White House made a public statement to that effect. Again, it was my unofficial status that made it possible to negotiate because the United States had a policy in Haiti of not allowing our ambassador in Port-au-Prince to communicate with the officials in Haiti who had replaced Aristide. So the bottom line is that although I go with the sometimes grudging approval of the White House, I never do go without that approval.

HIR: Returning again to the examples of North Korea, Bosnia, and Haiti that you have mentioned, you have maintained in the past that to resolve a crisis it is often necessary to revisit recrimination and preserve strict neutrality. Some people have criticized your negotiations with leaders like Raoul Cédras or Radovan Karadžić as a demonstration of moral indifference or appeasement. How do you respond to this criticism?

JC: I do not forgo recrimination. I make it very clear that we condemn human rights violations, violations of democracy, the overthrow of a legitimately elected president like Aristide, and, obviously, Kim Il-sung's move toward establishing a nuclear arsenal. But at the same time, I go to visit with these leaders and see what we can do to correct the problems faced. In most cases the leaders are quite eager to work out a disharmony with the United States and sometimes, in the case of North Korea, with the entire world. They need someone who will go there and listen and talk, and give them advice and be honest with them, and that is what I do. They still know that I am a strong advocate of human rights and that I deplore the actions they have taken. Although they have been guilty sometimes of crimes or mistakes, the most important objective is to make sure that the crimes are terminated and that the mistakes are corrected. And sometimes that means talking with people in an unofficial way, something that no one else is able or willing to do.

HIR: How would you set the balance between justice and peace in a situation in which concessions to people whom we would consider political criminals are necessary to ensure peace and stability?

JC: You can never overlook the aspect of justice. For example, we have been deeply involved in the problems with Rwanda and Burundi, and we publicly demand that the international tribunal be honored and that any leaders indicted for war crimes or for genocide be delivered to the tribunal. I have always maintained the same position in the case of Bosnia-Herzegovina, so I think that the element of justice cannot be ignored. It would be much easier for me to go into the refugee camps outside of Rwanda and mediate with the Hutu refugees, some of whom are guilty of genocide, but they know that our policy is that they must be punished if they are found guilty of genocide.

In Haiti, the choice between justice and peace was never directly addressed by the US government or the United Nations. We complied completely with the provisions of the negotiations between Aristide and Cédras and with the agreement worked out at Governor's Island in New York between those leaders. Also, there were two UN Security Council resolutions that addressed the actions of Cédras and his associates. None of those agreements or resolutions called for a trial or for punishment of the leaders; they called for Cédras to step down from his office and to permit Aristide to return to Haiti peacefully. That is what we negotiated. In addition, we made arrangements for Cédras and his family to leave Haiti and go to Panama. But in none of the cases in which we have been involved did we circumvent, or advocate against, punishment for crimes that were committed.

HIR: Moving on to another topic, on last year's fiftieth anniversary of the United Nations you made several suggestions for UN reform, including perhaps the eventual creation of a UN military force, expansion of the Security Council, and a reassessment of the US share of the overall financial burden. What is the potential for the implementation of these reforms?

JC: The worst single problem is that the United States refuses to pay its dues, so in all the UN agencies, even UNICEF, the voice of the United States is almost completely mute. We are now probably one and a half billion dollars in arrears. We go into the Security Council and vote for a peacekeeping effort, and we sometimes lead the fight to get the peacekeeping effort approved, and then we refuse to help pay for it. What the United States is doing is a disgrace.

I have also advocated some expansion of the membership of the Security Council. The total dominance of the Security Council over the United Nations and the veto power held by the five permanent members is now passé. In addition, I think a permanent peacekeeping force, made up almost exclusively of small countries that are not superpowers, would be very good. As I said, fifty years ago when the United Nations was created, it was designed to prevent another world war, but now there are thirty-one major civil wars in the world. UN peacekeeping forces would be ideal to address these kinds of war. A small cadre of troops, once they receive training, could even be stationed in their own countries but be available on short notice for dispatch to a place like Rwanda or Liberia, when the urgent need arises. Otherwise, it takes many weeks to get a resolution through the Security Council and then to organize such a peacekeeping force. The cost would be minimal compared to what we now have to pay to marshal a force to respond to an emergency at the last minute. Some nations might place certain restrictions on the involvement of their troops; the United States might, for example, insist that any US troops be commanded by a US general. For that reason, the permanent troops should come from the small countries, not from the United States, Russia, Great Britain, France, Germany, or other powerful nations.

HIR: One region in which consolidating the peace is a very prominent issue is, of course, the Middle East. In light of your long-standing experience in conflict resolution in the Middle East, from the Camp David accords during your term as president to such recent efforts as the monitoring of the Palestinian elections, what do you see as the greatest challenges to peace in the Middle East? What can be done to enable supporters of peace to overcome resistance from their own side?

JC: The first and most crucial challenge is to get the peace process back on track. Beginning in May, for instance, the Israelis and the Palestinians were supposed to raise the long-term questions about the return of refugees, the exact delineation of the boundary between Israel and the Palestinian area, and the release of prisoners, but that has now been delayed because Israel has delayed removing its troops from Hebron.

The second challenge, in my opinion, is to search out the moderate leaders among the Palestinians, even in Hamas, who are willing to forego violence and join in the peace process. When I went over to monitor the Palestinian election in January, I met with some Hamas leaders, and I asked them to pledge to me that they would not use violence during the election. They made this commitment to me and they carried out that limited promise. Although I cannot say whether they were telling the truth, they said that they were very eager to meet with Arafat and other leaders, including those from Israel, to work out a proper role for Hamas to play. That would still leave some extremists among the Palestinians outside the scope of mediation, but I think that some exploration should be made among Hamas and other Palestinian groups who do not agree with Arafat to determine how they could play a constructive role.

And the third challenge, which has unfortunately been pushed the forefront too many times, is the peace agreement between Israel and Syria. For the past ten years there has been no fighting between Syrian and Israeli troops, but we have wasted an enormous amount of time trying to get Hafez al-Assad and the Israeli prime minister to agree to a settlement. I heard on National Public Radio this past month that Secretary of State Warren

Christopher has been over in the Middle East working on the Syrian problem at least seventeen different times since he has been in office; yet he has never been to Liberia, Sudan, Rwanda, or Burundi, which shows a displaced priority. Of course it is important to pursue peace in the Middle East, and Secretary Christopher deserves much credit for mediating the recent understanding between Israel, Lebanon, and Syria, but there needs to be a balance so that other regions are not neglected.

HIR: What are some of those regions that you believe have received inadequate attention in US foreign policy?

JC: In Africa alone there are several problems. The Rwanda and Burundi issue is perhaps the worst problem in the world: in the last thirty months, one hundred thousand people were killed in Burundi, and more than five hundred thousand Rwandans were killed in 1994 while two million more went into exile that year. That is one problem to which the Carter Center and I are devoting most of our time. Liberia is another crucial issue, and the civil fighting there is very destabilizing to the other fifteen West African nations. A third problem is Sudan, where more than one and a half million people have been killed in the ongoing civil war. We did negotiate a peace there last year, which was originally for only two months but lasted more than six months. Nothing is being done officially to negotiate a peace agreement in Sudan. Another very serious matter concerns Somalia. The world has turned away from Somalia, and now we have five warlords, each of whom leads his own troops and his own political organization, squabbling with each other. Nothing is being done to try to mediate among those five to restore peace in Somalia. So just in the northern part of Africa there are these four major problems that are not being addressed.

HIR: Given that there are such problems, which traditional organizations like the United Nations and national governments are not addressing, do you see a rise in nongovernmental activity? If there is greater "political space" to undertake humanitarian initiatives in today's world, will traditional organizations eventually be able to take over the work of NGOs?

JC: NGOs generally function only when governments or other official bodies cannot or will not. The Carter Center has a policy of not going anywhere except to fill a vacuum. If the United Nations or the US government or the World Bank or others are doing something about a certain issue, we do not try to duplicate their efforts. We go mostly to crisis areas where little or nothing is being done. I am very eager for the United Nations to take over our responsibility in the Rwanda-Burundi area of Africa, for example, once the leaders of the five nations involved agree to UN involvement. It is not easy for me to raise enough money to undertake the discussions alone, which is one of the main problems faced by NGOs.

The United Nations and governments, particularly the US government, sometimes resent the initiatives undertaken by NGOs. But countries such as Norway encourage NGOs to take a leadership role. When the peace was negotiated between the Israeli government and the Palestinians, a completely unofficial social science group in Norway helped bring about the Oslo agreement in cooperation with the Norwegian Foreign Ministry. There is a very great needs to expand the capabilities of NGOs to fill these vacuums in international humanitarian affairs and conflict mediation.

A Former President Warns of "Endangered Values"

Terry Gross / 2005

Fresh Air with Terry Gross, WHYY, November 2, 2005 edition. Reprinted with the permission of WHYY, Inc. *Fresh Air with Terry Gross* is produced by WHYY in Philadelphia and distributed by NPR.

Terry Gross: Jimmy Carter was the first American president to tell the public that he was born again. But he believes in the separation of church and state, and is worried that the wall is eroding. In his new book, *Our Endangered Values*, he draws on his experiences as president and as a Baptist to explain his concerns about the intertwining of politics and religion. President Carter, welcome back to *Fresh Air*. Do you think the line between church and state has shifted since you were president?

Jimmy Carter: Well, this separation of church and state which Thomas Jefferson ordained, as a wall between the two, has been severely breached in the last fifteen or twenty years and in particular, the last five years. So the answer is yes.

When I was president I, and I think all my predecessors and most of my successors, have been meticulous in trying to separate church and state and not inject religious aspects into policy, and not let the churches or any religion dominate or heavily influence the political decisions made by this government. So this is a radical departure from what we've seen in our country since its founding.

Gross: Are there times where you feel President [George W.] Bush has eroded the line between church and state?

Carter: Oh, yes, I don't think there's any doubt that the nation knows that President Bush [. . .] strongly favors the religious right, Protestant Christians in our country. There's no doubt about this, in my opinion. But the religious part is not the most important—I think that's the background of the foundation for a lot of changes—but the major changes that concern me are more secular in nature.

For us, we have always had a policy in our country of peace that is in our country would not go to war and attack another country, bomb its people invade that nation, unless our own security was directly threatened. That's been abandoned under this administration, and now the new policy is preemptive war, which the president declared at West Point as you know, a couple of years ago. Our country now because of its tremendous military might reserves a right, publicly declared, to invade another country to attack another country and to kill its citizens—not if our nation's security is in danger, but if we want to change the regime there for some reason.

We've also abandoned our longstanding and admirable commitment to civil liberties and personal privacy of Americans, and the protection of human rights around the world. This has not only been a matter of great pride to America, but it's also compatible with international law. And we now see a struggle within the Congress at this moment to permit the CIA, for instance, to torture prisoners. This is in direct violation of longstanding principles of our country, moral values, and also in direct violation of international agreements. So the radical change in America's domestic and international policies are what I'm trying to cover in saying that our endangered values are America's moral crisis and around the world.

Gross: You were the first president to say that you were born again. You said that during the election when you were asked by a reporter. After you proclaimed that you were born again, how did that change perceptions of you?

Carter: It was a very serious mistake for me to make. I was actually in the backyard of a friend in North Carolina. And I was asked: "Are you a born-again Christian?" And I answered, truthfully, "Yes, I am."

I had always assumed that that phrase was completely acceptable, at least among Christians. And there were news reporters there—it was kind of late in the '76 campaign—and it was reported and the reaction was very severe and negative because the people who are not familiar with that phrase had assumed that I was claiming to have some special endowment from God and visions. And I also tended to elevate myself above all other human beings in my moral standards, which was not the case at all.

Being a born-again Christian was a phrase I used since I was probably three or four years old, as used readily in Christian churches in my area. So it was a very negative reaction to what I had to say. And I was very careful from then on to separate, openly and ostentatiously, my religious faith from any responsibilities that I assumed when I became president.

Gross: How active do you think the Christian right was in 1976?

Carter: They were nonexistent. They were really nonexistent then. There were a few statements made from some people that would now be called the Christian right, but they were insignificant. I think it was probably three or four years later, before I think *Time*—or *Newsweek* magazine, I've forgotten—had a front cover story on the on the birth of the of the Christian right.

And in my own denomination, I was a Southern Baptist. It was the election of a president of the Southern Baptist Convention in 1979 that brought about a change in our own denomination. It took ten years or so to completely implement what they espoused as fundamentalist. But it was not culminated until the year 2000. And at that time, a new doctrine was established in the Southern Baptist Convention like a creed, and that creed has now been imposed on Baptists, and of course, Baptists have been noncreedal people since the founding of our faith many, many years ago. But those were the changes that have taken place.

Gross: When you were president, did you ever find that your political position and your religious views ever came into conflict?

Carter: Yes. There was one issue in particular that was a very serious problem for me, and that was abortion. I have never believed that Jesus Christ whom I worship would approve abortions, unless the mother's health or life was threatened or perhaps if the pregnancy was from rape or incest. This is hard for me to accept.

And at the same time, I was sworn by oath to uphold the laws and constitution of United States as interpreted by the Supreme Court. And the Supreme Court had ruled that some abortions in the first semester of pregnancy were completely acceptable. So I tried to do everything I could, within the bounds of the law, to minimize and discourage abortions. As a matter of fact, one of the easily understood principles, is that two thirds of the women who have abortions claim, at least, that the reason is that they cannot financially support another child. So I developed what's known as Women and Children's program—WIC program—to give special benefits to women and infants and pregnant women and infant children. Also, I promoted the proposition that adoption should be easier, and I tried to promulgate training for in high school on ways to avoid unwanted pregnancy.

But I had to uphold the law, so that particular one was troublesome for me. Another that was legally troublesome for me, that didn't really ever come into effect, was a Supreme Court ruling shortly before I became president that authorized a death penalty that had been prohibited as unfair. But when the Supreme Court ruled, luckily, I went through my entire term as governor and my entire term as president, and no one was executed under my administrations. And I have never felt that Jesus Christ, again, would approve the death penalty, or as it's personally supported so strongly by some of the conservative Christians and others in this country. Those are the two issues.

Gross: With abortion, since you personally oppose abortion but upheld a woman's right to abortion because the Supreme Court ensured that right, did you ever state your views on abortion? Do you feel like you should speak out against abortion as you continued to uphold the right to abortion?

Carter: Yes, I did frequently. As a matter of fact, I covered this in the book. On one occasion, I was questioned, at one of my very frequent White House press conferences, about the fact that rich women could buy abortions and that poor women didn't have a right to an abortion unless the federal government paid for them. And I made the remark that was somewhat criticized—and I can see why—that sometimes life is unfair.

That's not a very good statement for a president to make, but that was the way I felt. I didn't think it was right for our country to support abortions by paying for abortions, if it was just to end a pregnancy when the mother's life or safety was not in danger.

[. . .]

Gross: You mentioned that when you publicly stated that you were born-again when you were running for president, that it worked against you; people misunderstood what you meant by that, and you thought it hurt you in the election. It's funny because, as you know, President Bush is born-again. He discussed that when he was running for office, and it seemed to help him very much in his campaign. So would you reflect a little bit about what's changed?

Carter: Well, what's changed is what I described earlier, that is, the rise of fundamentalism has affected both politics—including national policy—in domestic and foreign affairs, and also has affected the religious community much more than it ever did when I was in politics, and the two have now merged. So there is an ostentatious and very aggressive effort among the, you might say, religious right leaders, and I don't criticize them because of their beliefs publicly to align themselves with the Republican Party, provided the Republican Party members they may support are adequately conservative. So that marriage has been a radical departure, in my opinion, from the ancient values of our country.

At the same time to various means, some of them not well publicized, there has been a tremendous amount of taxpayers money that is being sent directly to churches in our country, and the argument has been: can the churches be discriminatory against people who receive services through them from taxpayers' money? And the present administration's policy is that we should not make the churches declare nondiscrimination, let them discriminate. So these two factors are unprecedented in our country, and I think they contravene the basic premises on which our country was founded as espoused, most clearly, by Thomas Jefferson who advocated a wall between church and state.

Gross: You're a Baptist and you say in your book that Southern Baptists had been committed to the separation of church and state, and that the church abhorred the concept of churches becoming involved in the partisan world and this is when you were growing up. Why was that, there, that rejection of getting involved in in the political partisan world?

Carter: Well, when I was a little child, my father was a Sunday school teacher and it was inculcated in me and other students then that the basic origins of the Baptist Church in this country was in independence from government, and that we would not abide by government ordaining a particular denomination or particular faith or particular church to be to be dominant, as has happened in Europe, and that's why a lot of people came over. Roger Williams founded our church in this particular country.

Also, the Baptists have always been a noncreedal organization, and that means that not only is every individual church congregation autonomous or sovereign, but that every individual human being has a right to go directly to God through prayer, and to relate directly with God. So we avoided any sort of creed to be imposed on us by an outside power.

And the Southern Baptist Convention itself has now departed from that and in the year 2000, as I mentioned earlier, adopted a very severe creed that now must be adopted, officially, by anyone who serves as a pastor in a church, who serves as a missionary overseas, who has a job as administrator or teacher in one of the Southern Baptist conventions or seminaries to teach students, and so forth. So we have departed, I'm afraid in many ways, from those religious policies.

Gross: You and Rosalynn left the Southern Baptist conference. Was it because of this new creed?

Carter: Yes, because of a new creed and some of the elements of it.

Two things that I didn't mention that caused me concern was in the old standards that Baptists used to use, very lax, it said that the interpretation of biblical verses—there are more than 30,000 of them—would be, for Christians, the words and actions of Jesus Christ. That statement was deleted from a new creed and instead, and obviously in effect, the elected leaders of the Southern Baptist Convention would then be the interpreters of the Scripture. And all subordinates, all people who adhere to that, had had to agree.

The other thing was their declaration concerning the subservience of women, that women have to be subservient to their husbands. And there now is a prohibition against any woman occupying a position of authority or responsibility within the Southern Baptist Convention. Our most famous and revered heroes when I was a child were people like Lottie Moon, who was a missionary to China; we still give a Lottie Moon Christmas offering throughout the Southern Baptist Convention. Now a woman can't be the lead missionary; a woman can't even be a chaplain for us just now, in the military forces, if she's a Southern Baptist. They have just about those policies, that a woman can't speak with authority or teach men in a church. Those are just a couple of the of a newly ordained principles that all Southern Baptists now have to accept in order to be a member of the convention. I can't, and couldn't, agree to that.

Gross: What about the church that you've belonged to in Plains, Georgia for so long? The church in which you've taught Sunday school for so many years? Are the members of that church still members of the Southern Baptist Convention?

Carter: I think, if I'm not mistaken, almost all of the members of our church agree with me, and what I've just described to you as basic religious principles, the sainthood of the believer, that is that each individual has a right to worship God directly, that each church has to be autonomous. We have women deacons, and next month we will ordain a woman minister in our church. She will be the associate minister of our church. And we believe that we shouldn't be bound by a creed imposed on us by outside, so the members of my church, still a Baptist church, have the same beliefs that I do, in fact. I can't say that everybody is 100 percent in agreement with me, but we have open discussions when our congregation gets together, and I think I'm accurately expressing the overwhelming beliefs.

[. . .]

Gross: Let me ask you about evolution, since Intelligent Design is before the courts now. How do you deal with the fact that science tells us different things than the Bible does, about the creation of men and women and the Earth?

Carter: Well, in the *Our Endangered Values* book, I describe my feelings about this quite thoroughly. I studied nuclear physics when I was a young man; I was one of the originators of a nuclear submarine program. I worked under Admiral Hyman Rickover. At the same time, as you've already mentioned, I'm a devout Christian. I don't see any incompatibility at all between the two.

My belief is that God created the universe. My belief is that God permits us to understand the new developments that we can witness in universal matters. When the Bible was written, we didn't have the Hubble telescope. We didn't have microscopes so we could look at small items. We didn't have a way to test the age of rocks and so forth, but now we have these scientific capabilities. I think that science is just a revelation of God's creation, and so that the two are completely separate. And we can't prove the existence of things in our faith. As a matter of fact, the definition of faith in the Bible is that we know things that cannot be proven.

But we don't have to have faith to believe that the moon is out there; that's something that we can see for ourselves. And we can't have science prove the existence of God, all of the things that we know about Jesus Christ as a Christian. So the two are separate. I don't believe there's any place in a scientific classroom to try to prove to the students that God exists. I think the two ought to be completely separate, and one should not be imposed on the other.

[. . .]

Gross: You write in your book that you think one of the most bizarre mixtures of religion and government is the strong influence of some Christian fundamentalists on US policy in the Middle East. And you're referring there to Christians who believe in the rapture, that the Second Coming of Jesus is imminent, and that those who are born again will ascend to heaven when the Second Coming arrives, and everyone else will be left behind to face the tribulations. And Israel is important in this formula. What is Israel's place in this?

Carter: Well, what the people believe that you've just described is that Israel must take over the complete Holy Land, which is Gaza and all the West Bank so that the temple on the mount, for instance, can be destroyed, and temple of Israel replace it, and other matters of that kind. And then in the end, when the rapture occurs and the chosen people by God had been taken miraculously and instantaneously to heaven, and all the rest of us all of us, or them, will be condemned to Hades. At that time, all the Jews, according to this principle, will either be converted to Christianity or burned. And so the ultimate goal of these people, the ultimate belief of these people—I'm sure they're very sincere and devout—is that that Judaism will be terminated completely, and that every Jew will have to be a Christian or have to die. Well, I think that the some of the Jewish leaders are willing to accept the proposition that Jews take over the West Bank and colonize the entire area of Palestinian land, but they don't look at the final premise on which this philosophy is based.

Gross: So you're surprised that there are Israelis and Jewish American supporters, who are forming alliances with the Christian right?

Carter: I'm not surprised. I think that they are willing to take this financial help and this encouragement, for some of the more conservative Jewish leaders, to colonize the West Bank, and I think they just ignore as a fallacy, an unproven premise that ultimately, they will suffer either death or have to become a Christian. I think they're ignoring the ultimate consequence, under the belief that it's probably not going to happen, but they're willing to take the immediate benefits.

Gross: After Hurricane Katrina destroyed some of the oil infrastructure along the Gulf Coast, President Bush made a speech in which he asked Americans to turn down their thermostats and carpool and do other things to conserve energy. And when you made your time to conserve energy speech, [when] you were president, people mocked you for it. And in fact, some people thought it contributed to your losing your reelection campaign. Can you talk a little bit about that speech, and what you were hoping to accomplish by giving it, and what your reaction was to the reaction you got after you gave it?

Carter: Well, I had to fight the oil crisis throughout my four years as president, and even when I was a governor, and President Richard Nixon was president, we had boycotts against the sale of oil to us because we were friendly toward Israel. And under President Nixon, and under me again, there were long lines at service stations waiting for gasoline. The last twelve months of my term, the price of oil skyrocketed—much, much greater increase than it has been in the last twelve months or so—because Iraq invaded Iran, and all the oil from Iraq and Iran was terminated from the world's supplies. So I was very seriously and adversely affected as an incumbent president, so was our nation, by our sustained crisis concerning oil.

My main thrust was to conserve oil, to conserve energy, and I worked out—just to give you one example, to save time, with the Congress and with the oil companies and primarily with automobile manufacturers, to require the increase of efficiency of automobiles from twelve miles per gallon when I became president. And we established in the law an increase to twenty-seven-and-a-half miles per gallon. When I went out of office inadvertently, and because of the 1980 election, that policy was basically terminated. And under President Reagan and his successors the requirement for efficient automobiles has been lost.

Now, of course, the big SUVs and hummers and so forth don't come on any sort of restraints at all. And American motor vehicles use about 40 percent of our total oil, and we become heavily dependent again on foreign oil. So that's what I had to struggle with, and that's what President Bush is addressing now. President Bush has not been willing to impose any kind of restraints on the efficiency of automobiles.

Gross: Let me get back to the speech. You wore a cardigan; everybody always mentions that when they mention the speech, "He was wearing a cardigan." You talked about the importance of turning down the thermostat and conserving energy. What did you think the reaction of the American public was going to be?

Carter: Well, as a matter of fact, if you look at the record, which I've done fairly often—[*chuckles*]—in the four years, we were able to impose into law a profoundly important set of standards for efficiency, for insulation of homes for the efficiency of stoves and refrigerators and other appliances, for electric motors used in industry, as well as the motor vehicles that I've described already to you. So despite the constant altercation about it, both Democrats and Republicans in the House and Senate approved my basic proposals, and we did implement those issues.

So my hope and my expectation when I made the speech, in my cardigan sweater, were realized, and when I left office there was a profoundly important set of laws imposed, and rules imposed, and most of them have survived. The efficiency requirements for electric motors and refrigerators, stoves, and houses still exist without any attenuation. The basic change has been in motor vehicles, and that's where the present administration has backed away as well as some of its predecessors.

Gross: President Carter, thank you for talking with us today. Thank you very much.

Carter: Terry, it's been a pleasure to be with you on *Fresh Air* again. It means a lot to me.

Exclusive Interview:
President Jimmy Carter

George C. Edwards III / 2008

Presidential Studies Quarterly 38.1 (March 2008). © Center for the Study of the
Presidency and Congress.

On May 18, 2007, I interviewed President Jimmy Carter in his office in the
Carter Center in Atlanta. The thirty-ninth president granted me an unusu-
ally long interview, excerpts from which are printed here.

George C. Edwards III: Mr. President, first, let me thank you for meeting with me today. I know that devoting an hour to an interview is unusual.
I am honored to have this opportunity, and our readers will be most grate-
ful for your insights. The first question I have is a broad one. I do not have
to tell you that there are great differences among the contexts of presiden-
cies in such fundamental aspects of politics as the state of the economy, the
party alignment in Congress, or the issues on the agenda. Richard Neustadt
once commented that it was silly that so many people in 1977 were using the
L. B. J. analogy of 1965 to think about your presidency. From your perspective as president, how did the context of your presidency affect you as you
set out to govern?

President Jimmy Carter: I had been governor when Nixon was in office
and part of the time when Johnson was there. I campaigned for a long time,
throughout 1975 and up until November 1976, in all fifty states. I had intimate
contacts with different constituencies, beginning with just tiny groups and
building as I gained popularity and fame. I had a very good opportunity to
learn from my choice of the most respected analysts or thinkers on the political scene, primarily those who related to the Democratic party. I would bring
busloads of key people down to Plains after I won the nomination, and after I
won the election, to give me intense briefings all day long, maybe forty or fifty

people at a time, on the economy, on the Panama Canal issue, on the Middle East, or on relationships with Russia and China? Whatever I wanted.

So I was thoroughly familiar with the issues when I finally was inaugurated. Before that, I worked very intimately with Dr. Brzeziński in outlining roughly ten major goals that I wanted to accomplish while I was in the White House.

I was minimally affected by what Johnson had done or Kennedy had done, although I was aware of it. My hero among my predecessors was Harry Truman. I thought he epitomized what I wanted to be as a president. I was heavily affected by his ordaining an end to racial segregation in the military, years before Rosa Parks sat in the front row of the bus or Martin Luther King was known.

Maybe I was overly confident when I was inaugurated about what I could do. I recognize that my positions were somewhat of an anomaly in that I was not compatible with the Kennedy regime, the liberal wing of the party. I was not compatible with the Richard Russell and Walter George constituency in the South. I was very progressive on social issues and very conservative on balancing the budget and on a strong military. That created a quandary in the assessments by news reporters and columnists and, I guess, by many of the people with whom I had to work in Congress.

I deliberately chose Walter Mondale to be my running mate because he and I were compatible personally, but also because I wanted somebody that was younger and progressive and was familiar with the congressional scene. Hubert Humphrey was kind of a hero of mine as well, so that is why I went ultimately toward Walter Mondale.

I had a pretty clear concept of what I wanted to accomplish when I went to the White House. I heard a cacophony of voices in dealing with some of the major issues that I would face. Energy, for instance, was one. I had been immersed in education matters before I got into politics when I was a state senator, and when I was governor. I saw the need, for instance, to create new departments for Energy and Education. I brought them together, I think thirty-three agencies into Energy? I cannot remember exactly, and I made Education a separate entity.

I was taken aback in my first few days in the White House. I could not get a single Democrat to sponsor my legislation that I wanted for reorganizing the government, legislation that gave me authority to reorganize and then Congress authority to veto what I did. So I had to go to Republicans to introduce my first bill in the House of Representatives. I never considered myself, even in retrospect, to be reluctant to turn to the Republicans to help me, and that was pretty well established my first week in the White House.

Later, Ted Kennedy, who was my number one supporter on a percentage basis the first year I was in the White House, decided to replace me as the Democratic party's nominee, and he and Senator Byrd formed a coalition. From then on, I was faced with a schism that increasingly separated me from the liberal wing of the Democratic party. But I had strong support among Republicans, and Howard Baker turned out to be my key contact within the US Senate.

What I inherited from my predecessors shaped my agenda. I can list four or five examples. One of them was the Panama Canal treaties which I saw as a potentially explosive factor in this entire hemisphere. In fact, the Group of 77, as you know, unanimously condemned the United States, and we lost a good relationship with Latin American countries. I was, I think naively, committed to consummating a new Panama Canal treaty.

The Mideast peace process was a religious commitment of mine. I had been to the Mideast as governor, and I felt that up until I took over that there had not been an effort for a comprehensive peace proposal, although Nixon and Kissinger had ended the 1973 war with cease-fires.

I had been in China when I was a young officer. I was fascinated with China, and I studied George Marshall's policies and that sort of thing. I went to China in 1949, the same year that the Nationalists left the mainland. I wanted to build on what Nixon had done. He said there was one China, but he never would say whether it was Taiwan or the mainland. Gerald Ford ignored the Chinese issue. Ronald Reagan was attacking Ford from the right wing to put potential progress on China on hold. I was determined to normalize relations with China.

Federal energy policy had cast a blight on my governorship, which was during the time when members of OPEC had an embargo against our country and a secondary boycott against American corporations that traded with Israel. I saw that and thought it was a disgrace.

The environment issue was also important to me. When I became governor, I was faced with two major crises. One of them was the damming up the Flint River. There were two major dams that had been approved that were completely unnecessary and counterproductive, but they were sponsored by a very prominent congressman from Griffin, Georgia. The other one was the draining of wetlands. There were some 590 wetlands-draining proposals in process of being approved automatically when I became governor. I vetoed every one of them, and since then there has not been one approved in Georgia.

I was immersed in that issue. I saw the environment as a major challenge for me.

I inherited the Alaska statehood legislation from Dwight Eisenhower, where for twenty years or so nobody had been willing to resolve the issue of land allotments in Alaska.

These issues inherited from my predecessors were long overdue for substantive treatment. I was not dismayed by them, but I was challenged to resolve them. I think going down that list in retrospect we basically resolved them all while I was in office.

I think some of them have reemerged.

That puts it in context. Every president inherits unresolved issues. I think almost every one of mine in foreign affairs would go back either to the founding of Israel, or to the Cold War confrontation with the Soviet Union, or to the first Panama Canal treaty.

Edwards: Now let me move to something more specific and that is relations with the public, certainly one of the primary presidential relations. You often asked the American public to face their problems squarely and sometimes to make sacrifices, like turning down heat to save on energy, and you spoke dramatically about a crisis of confidence. The same kinds of general principles seem relevant today, talking about funding Social Security in the long term, energy again, and environmental protection, for example. So I would like your view on how well can a president convince the public to face a potential crisis before it actually hits or does it take events to capture the public's attention and to educate it?

Carter: It takes both. Events can sometimes force a president to face a crisis that is already there and sometimes a cognizant president can anticipate a crisis and try to prepare the public for it or induce the public to help prepare for it by making some moderate sacrifices.

I think that in the case of energy it was more than just turning down the heat. There was a gamut of what I would guess were ten or twelve major issues that faced me concerning energy, and I think the first year I was in office I made four major speeches to the public on energy. Some of them fell on deaf ears, but eventually we got almost all that we wanted while I was in office, with more efficient motors, generators, refrigerators, stoves, automobiles, and house insulation.

The most difficult thing there, that I got by I think two votes, was the deregulation of the price of oil, which had been pegged at an extremely, abnormally low price. This was an issue that brought me in conflict with the oil companies, because we had windfall profit tax attached to it so the increase in price of oil could not result in their increased profits. At the same time, it was inevitably going to increase the price of gasoline and natural gas to consumers. We finally got that passed. I need not go into detail about what the deleterious effects of that excessively low price had been in the past, but it encouraged Americans to waste energy. If I remember right, we were importing about nine million barrels of oil per day. I thought that was a danger to us, because it permitted the oil suppliers to intercede not only in our international affairs but also in our domestic affairs, as had been demonstrated by the secondary boycotts against American corporations—which we outlawed by the way.

Over a period of five or six years, a couple of years into the Reagan administration, we went from nine million down to five million. We are back up to twelve million now.

That was an important issue for me, and a very difficult one. I never was successful in convincing the American public that they should join in with me wholeheartedly. Although we lowered the speed limit to fifty miles an hour, which was a big issue, particularly in places like Montana or Wyoming. And we built upon a law that was passed under Ford to require automobiles to become more efficient, which was undone by Reagan. We set as a goal 20 percent renewable energy sources—solar, wind power—and I do not need to go into detail about that. Within five years we increased renewable energy sources from I think about 6 percent when I was in office up to 9 percent. Now it is back down to about 6 percent, but we wanted to go to 20 percent.

Those are major goals. One thing that made it difficult for me and for my image was that we set very high publicized standards for what I wanted to have, say 100 percent. We would have an intense debate with Congress on a bipartisan basis. We would get 75 percent of what we wanted, which is 75 percent more than we had to start with, but the image was that we lost 25 percent. I am not complaining about that, but that is a truism of politics. I do not think there is any doubt that a president can expedite the public's view to avoid a crisis if he is wise and willing to take a chance, but sometimes his best efforts are fruitless.

Edwards: Let me ask a follow-up on that. Presidents, of course, spend a lot of time trying to convince the public to support their policies, themselves, or both. They often fail. Under what conditions is a president most likely to be able to move public opinion?

Carter: It is when evidence external from the White House corroborates what the president's message is. When that does occur, then of course the president's message can be more effective. In 1979, we had a repetition of gas lines at pumps, particularly when Iraq invaded Iran, and you might say we lost all the exported oil from those two major oil suppliers. So I think that helped me get the final stages, not 100 percent, of what we attempted to do in the energy legislation. So that was evidence that corroborated what I was saying.

A "moral equivalent of war" may have been an excessive statement. I derived that from my mentor, Admiral Hyman Rickover, who referred to the energy crisis in those terms. I was influenced heavily by Rickover. After I left the submarine force, in most years Rickover would write a treatise on something, I would say maybe twenty or thirty pages double-spaced, and he would send it to his officers and former officers. He wrote a treatise once of the energy issue while I was still governor. He made it so that I could understand it for the first time. Instead of saying a quadrillion BTUs or hundreds of millions of barrels of oil, he described the oil reserves in cubic miles. Plains is a circle a half a mile in diameter, and I could envision Plains being a mile deep in oil. Anybody can envision what a cubic mile is. At that time the total world reserves were about twenty-one cubic miles, and we were using up so many cubic miles a year. So he explained that to me.

But anyway, I got the "moral equivalent of war" from Rickover, and the issue obsessed me. It took up more of my time, more of my energy, and more of my access to the news media, more of my speech efforts than any other issue during my entire administration.

Edwards: That is fascinating. Let me ask you one other thing about a president's relations with the public, and that is about your election in 1976. The results were pretty close. As far as Congress's responsiveness to you or your own assessment of whether you had a mandate, did it matter that your margin of victory was small?

Carter: I don't believe the closeness affected me. I have seen some statements lately that I am the only Democratic candidate since Johnson who actually received a majority of the votes.

This is a brief recapitulation. When I first got the nomination and Ford got the nomination, the Republican party was deeply split between Ford and Reagan, and a lot of the Republicans in the public opinion polls said they were not going to vote for Ford.

So it made my margin of preference greatly exaggerated, I would say at least 15 percent when I got the nomination. We saw that. I did, and Hamilton Jordan did. All of us saw that as an exaggerated lead over Ford. And then as the time for the election approached, those Republican Reagan votes all went to Ford, which was predictable.

I won by a very small margin, but I never was constrained by the fear that I did not have a mandate.

Edwards: Did your margin of victory affect Congress at all?

Carter: I don't really know. The greatest incompatibility I had during the campaign was with the Democratic party. The Democratic party was never mine, and I accept a major part of the responsibility. I was doing great in public opinion polls, as a peanut farmer coming out of Georgia, as a non-lawyer, as one who had not been involved in Vietnam and Watergate. Then, when I actually got the nomination, I was saddled with the full responsibility for every Democratic candidate in America as a running mate. The more unattractive they were or the more obnoxious they were, the more they clung to me in my popularity to help them. It dragged me down. I am not complaining about that, that is part of life.

Even during the next four years, I was never able to consolidate support in the Democratic party, particularly after Kennedy decided to run for president. I think he sapped away about 5 or 6 percent of my votes in 1980.

I don't think that the narrowness of my victory over Ford adversely affected my relationship with the Congress. As a matter of fact, I have seen the congressional quarterly assessments, and in essence we had as good a batting average as Johnson or Kennedy as far as my proposals and the percentage being approved by the Congress.

Edwards: I would like to move on to what is probably the core function of the president, which is making decisions. We often do not think about decision making. We think about the individual decisions instead. Yet the style and process of decision making comes back to haunt us time and time again when bad decisions are made.

So I want to start with what I call details and decisions and a basic quandary of presidents. On the one hand, they are to set a broad vision for the country and for their administration. On the other hand, they need to reach down for tangible details of policy options so they understand them and can make wise decisions.

You are known for your mastery of complex policy, and you are interested in the details of policy as a good policy analyst. Other presidents have been less interested in details. So let me ask you into how much detail should a president delve in making decisions?

Carter: All of my answers are subjective, of course. I feel that in retrospect, and I also felt at the time, that we set strategic goals before I got to the White House. You can look at a speech I made at the Woodrow Wilson Center where I outlined ten things that I wanted to do in foreign policy—Mideast peace, Panama Canal treaties, normalize relations with China, for example. That is what I considered to be the strategic thinking. I won't go into domestic issues to save time. As time went on, I modified that list with changing circumstances and unanticipated challenges like the taking of hostages.

I really relished the strategic planning sessions that I had with Brzeziński every morning and habitually, without deviation, with my key advisors every Friday morning for an hour and a half. This is something I tried to get Clinton to do, but he never would. I had my national security adviser, the secretary of defense, the secretary of state, the vice president, and usually Hamilton Jordan and Jody Powell. Brzeziński was kind of a secretary. They would bring every issue that we were facing at that time or might come up on their distant horizons as a challenge. We discussed it in an open hour-and-a-half long breakfast in the Cabinet Room.

I would listen to all of those disparate voices, particularly differences such as those between Cy Vance and Brzeziński, and I would make a decision, and Brzeziński would write down my decision. Sometimes I would postpone a decision until the following week, but that would be kind of a maximum.

On Wednesday at noon Brzeziński, the secretary of defense, and the secretary of state would meet, and Brzeziński would assess how they were coming in carrying out my decisions. They would also prepare the agenda for the next Friday. We did that every week.

So on the big things, the strategic plans, I had a cacophony of voices before me, and I would make the decisions. Brzeziński was my best advisor, not State. When I needed innovative ideas, State was practically worthless. I say this in my book, *Keeping Faith*.

Regarding the details, I am still an engineer by thought. You know, when I run my farm or when I run the Carter Center, I want to know what is going on. When I took on the personal responsibility, say for the Mideast peace process, I really believed that when we went to Camp David I knew more about the details than anybody there. I had mastered the psychological and historical analysis of Begin and Sadat. I knew everything they had done since they were born that was recorded, how they had reacted to crisis, how they dealt with pressure, who their allies were, and what their obligations were. So when we got to Camp David, I knew them, and I knew the map of the West Bank and Gaza.

The first day or two when I negotiated with Begin and Sadat, Vance stayed in the little room and took notes, but later, after three days, Begin and Sadat were so incompatible that I kept them apart. They never saw each other for the last ten days. So I went back and forth. And I knew the issues, and I knew what I wanted.

I did basically the same thing with the Alaska Lands bill. I knew the map of Alaska in great detail. I read a lot. I would say I read an average of three hundred pages a day. That is just something that I quantified years ago, so I am not just talking casually. I took a speed-reading course. I did, and about fifty other people did, from Evelyn Wood in the Cabinet Room within the first two months of my term. So I could read a lot.

So, I studied those issues. In general, however, I limited the issues on which I was acquainted with the details to ones where I felt that I personally had to do the negotiating. I thought then, as I say this is a subjective analysis, that the major strategic concepts and goals that I wanted to set for myself were generically derived. But on a few issues I was very, highly informed personally.

Edwards: So it was particularly important to get into the great detail when you were personally negotiating?

Carter: Absolutely.

Edwards: That makes sense.

Carter: The most difficult issue I ever faced in my life, politically speaking, was the Senate ratification of the Panama Canal treaties. In the fall of 1976, forty-eight senators introduced a resolution in the Congress pledging not to approve any change in the Panama Canal treaties. I had to get sixty-seven affirmative votes. I called in senators to talk about the treaty, and each senator who was in opposition would have selected one particular sentence or paragraph in the Panama Canal treaties as written as their focal point for objection. They may have talked about that back in Nebraska or wherever. So I had to know the details of the Panama Canal treaties in order to sit down across from them in the Oval Office and try to convince them that their concerns were ill founded. It would have been much less effective if I would have had my secretary of state or Brzeziński present and turned to Brzeziński and asked him about a paragraph they were talking about.

Edwards: So you do not see any trade-off between vision and detail?

Carter: I do not think there is an incompatibility. The visions are the generic things, and you can give all of your subordinates the responsibility to carry those out. But there are a few things on which a president has got to be the key person.

I would presume that when Reagan was in office—I do not know this—that the senators or congressmen that he was trying to convince would come into the Oval Office and probably did not expect Reagan to know the details. It would have been more natural for him to turn to his secretary of defense, or state, or national security adviser to talk about details. We were just different persons. I am not criticizing him.

Edwards: I have a related question about delegation. There are many decisions that are made in government, and the president cannot make all of them. Sometimes presidents want to locate decisions in the White House, and sometimes they want to give lower officials discretion to make them—and they have to do that to some degree. When were you most comfortable in delegating decisions to subordinates?

Carter: I would say in domestic affairs I was most comfortable, because I had Stu Eisenstein in charge of my legislative drafting and domestic staff. If I wanted to prepare a proposal to the Congress concerning energy or the environment or welfare or health or education, I would just write a memo to Stu or talk to Stu and say this is what I want to do, and they would put together the detailed legislative proposals, and I would be perfectly at ease with that.

David Rubenstein was his assistant. He went on to become a great success and is now listed in the Forbes 400. But I never saw David much. He was always in the background. Stu had been an issue analyst when Hubert Humphrey ran for president in 1968.

He was from Georgia, and he was my issue analyst when I was campaigning. I was perfectly confident that when Stu and his staff came forward with a legislative proposal, it would comply with my overall instructions. So I did not need to study all the details to make sure they got it right.

Edwards: Very interesting. Now I would like to ask about another quandary. Leaders in every country and time period often become prisoners of their premises—and on the most significant matters—and make major mistakes. Prominent examples include the US before Pearl Harbor and the North Korean invasion of South Korea in 1950, Mao and famine in China, Hitler and the fortitude of the Soviet Union, the French general staff regarding the German strategy in both World War I and II—the list is endless. Every president comes into office with premises, views about the world and how it works and about policy. Every president has been thinking about these things for many years before arriving at the White House.

At the same time, commentators often argue that to make good decisions it is crucial to keep an open mind, to push back on advisors' advice, and to challenge one's premises, because these premises may be wrong and need to be adjusted or refined. The goal is to increase the probability of avoiding mistakes such as those that appear to have been made on the premises of the war with Iraq and the subsequent occupation. So the question is whether there is any formula for avoiding becoming a prisoner of your premises.

Carter: Yes, I think there is a way. First of all, choose top advisors in the cabinet and the national security staff who bring knowledge, diversity of opinion, and basic philosophy. A typical example, I need not to go into detail, would be Brzeziński and Vance. Then you need to make sure that you give their often conflicting views a fair hearing. Roosevelt is assessed to have done this overtly. I did it overtly. The *Washington Post* pointed it out just about every day.

I had a family—this is a footnote—my wife and my three sons who were out in the country every day during the campaign. That is why I won. We never campaigned together a single day. I won the campaign in 1976 because every Monday morning my wife, I, Jack and his wife, Chip and his wife, Jeff and his wife, my mother, and my mother's sister, seven of us, would go out to different places in America. We never went to the same place. We would campaign as best we could.

Every Saturday we would meet back at my house in Plains. We would spend Saturday afternoon going over our experiences, what people were saying in Iowa and how did it differ from what people were saying in Massachusetts, about abortion for instance, and so forth. We made sure that we were preaching the same sermon. On Sunday afternoons, at first we went to very small rallies and then larger and larger ones as my popularity increased. We would go where Hamilton Jordan and his staff suggested that we go. Hamilton and Jody and Frank Moore and others got together and said we think that the governor ought to go to Iowa and Mrs. Carter ought to go to Florida and that sort of thing.

We did that every week. By the time the other candidates woke up, they had lost. It was not my sterling character or my eloquence that did it. Rosalyn spent 105 days in Florida, and she went to 115 different communities in Iowa, in addition to what I did. The people knew us, and we all were giving the same message.

When I was president, Rosalyn and other family members were still traveling all over the country, and they would bring back to the White House, around the supper table, those disparate views. I was getting them also from others. So the first thing for a president who wants to avoid a generic mistake is to have diversity of opinions before making a decision. Then, it is important to be flexible enough to modify your preconceived ideas, which is not always easy, I admit.

I think that is one of the things that President Bush has not done. I am not criticizing him, but I think he has had almost a homogeneous cadre of people to whom he listened. I would guess that most other presidents have had more of an approach like I had.

So that would be a way, I think, to avoid being excessively committed to preconceived ideas.

Edwards: Another aspect of decision making, and another challenge for a president, is to get his advisors to tell him what he needs to hear as opposed to what they think he wants to hear. You are obviously a very intelligent person and you are a very competitive one, which is not unusual in presidents. Hamilton Jordan wrote in his memoirs that, if he wanted to change your mind on something that was important or complicated, he could not do it in person. He had to do it in writing, because as soon as he started talking, you would just overwhelm him with facts and analysis. So he never got to the second or the third point.

I merely add that anecdote for color, but the basic problem is every president faces a problem in ensuring that people tell him what he needs to hear and what they really think. We have plenty of examples of presidents who demeaned people who disagreed with them or closed out people who offered views they did not like or that were incompatible with their previous policy stances.

How did you make sure that you heard the full range of options? You mentioned earlier that you had open discussion on Friday mornings. So how did you make sure discussion was open so that people felt comfortable arguing with you or telling you things that you may not have thought at first?

Carter: The Friday morning example just applied to my national security advisers. But we had regular cabinet meetings, which were incisive discussions of issues that anybody wanted to bring up—concerning labor, or welfare, or housing, or the judiciary branch. We would go around the entire table, and I would encourage each secretary to tell me the most important things that affected their departments that we needed to discuss. I would presume that any of them that are still living would certify that I never restrained them from doing so. If the issue was complex and they required more than two or three minutes of exposition, I encouraged them to put it in writing and submit it to me. Those papers always came to me, and I relished that concise nature of their presentation. It required them to get their thoughts in order, and I was very much a stickler for not splitting infinitives and so forth.

And all of those papers are in the presidential library now. I think the scholars that have been over to the presidential library to look at my notes have been impressed, I started to say overwhelmed, with the meticulous detail with which I would answer sometimes each paragraph in a complex proposal—I approve this, I do not approve this, see me about this, or explain this, and so forth.

When I made a decision, I would expect everybody to comply or I gave everybody a chance for a reclama. Sometimes in domestic affairs or after the Friday morning meetings, if everybody spoke, and then I made a decision, and say if Cy Vance did not approve, I would give Cy a chance to come back later and give me the reasons why he disagreed with my decision. Vance threatened to resign three times, and one time he resigned, because we had some basic differences of opinion.

That is what I did to make sure that I got a complex and quite often diverse set of opinions.

Now there were some issues where I went against the majority. An overwhelming majority of my advisors said do not go to Camp David with the expectations of a comprehensive settlement. Even more vociferous was their objection to my going to Cairo and Jerusalem to consummate the peace treaty between Israel and Egypt. It was such a high-profile matter, that if I had failed, it would have been a devastating blow to my prestige and to the United States' prestige. But I went anyway.

Another example was the hostages being held in Iran. The vast majority of my advisors, including my most intimate ones, wanted me to take some military action against Iran. I could have done it, but I had a basic philosophy against the killing of innocent people. I felt, maybe more persuasively, that if I attacked Iran, they would very well assassinate all the hostages. I didn't know. So I refrained from that.

So that dragged the darn thing out for 444 days. If I had taken more incisive action, which I am sure George W. Bush would have done or maybe Bill Clinton, then it may have turned out differently.

But in most cases I went with the consensus.

Edwards: I would like to turn to Congress. In 1977, as you well know, you were criticized for being principled, for taking principled actions, particularly about the water projects. I think you will agree that some members of Congress were irritated by your stands.

Carter: There is no doubt about that. That is putting it mildly.

Edwards: And critics claimed that you were wasting precious political capital on these matters. When it came time for your major initiatives, of which there were several, how much do you think that this irritation mattered in obtaining congressional support?

Carter: It is hard for me to quantify the loss of votes because of the water project issue. It was impossible then or now. I would say that my immediate staff in the White House agreed with me. It was a seminal change in the status of the Army Corps of Engineers that was long overdue. It was the right thing to do.

I am not talking about individual projects, but the system as it evolved over maybe a century or more before I became president. What happened was that a member of Congress would go to Washington, and he or she would have a dam project that they wanted to see in their district, to dam up a pristine river to make a lake and so forth, which could be very attractive. Then the member would put the project on the list, and if that congressman survived for fifteen, twenty, twenty-five, or thirty years, their project would move up to the top and it would be automatically approved. The Corps of Engineers would deliberately falsify the cost versus benefit estimate to justify the project.

Well, those are the ones that I vetoed. I have to say that in good conscience, knowing what I knew and having been involved deeply in a major altercation in Georgia, which was precipitated by a lead article in *Reader's Digest* on the Flint River, I do not think I could have done differently. This is true even acknowledging the fact that I might lose certain votes from a congressman whose project I had vetoed. But how to quantify it, I don't know.

Edwards: In various interviews over the years, your aides have said that you really did not like to bargain with members of Congress. You liked figuring out what was the right thing to do and then proposing it or fighting for it rather than negotiating a compromise with Congress. In hindsight do you think that this orientation hindered your ability to obtain congressional support?

Carter: No, I don't think so. As I said earlier, this is a self-justification answer. If we could not get 100 percent and got 75 percent, what we bargained on was maybe that remaining 25 percent. But I would not bargain away a debilitating portion of what I wanted just to achieve an appearance of victory, which would have looked good maybe in the *Washington Post*— that Carter wins another victory. We never did—not to get a headline of that kind.

Even when we had major legislation adopted, the news media always emphasized the portions that I wanted that I did not get. So I can see that that may have in the long term been a deleterious impact on my political reputation or image.

I do not think I was excessively obdurate in my dealing with the Congress. I would guess that never in history has any president brought into the White House more members of Congress to listen to them and deal with them than I did. There were times when I brought in every member of the House, one hundred at a time, into the East Room. They would sit in nice chairs, and I would get in front and I would explain, or Stu Eisenstein or someone else would brief them on a complex issue such as foreign aid or energy and try to convince them to go my way.

There were other times when I brought in one member of Congress at a time, as I did trying to get US senators to vote for the Panama Canal treaties. When I had a senator, for instance, tell me privately, "I believe you are right on the Panama Canal Treaty, but I cannot support you because my people back home won't approve it," I would get a list of an average of 200 of his top fellow citizens—the owners of a TV station, the head of the VFW, college presidents, governors—and we would invite all of them to come to the White House. I and the key general in the Panama area and Brzeziński would give them a detailed briefing, and I would stay there for two hours answering their questions about the Panama Canal treaties. They would go back home and quite often the editorials in the paper would change.

That is how we finally prevailed. I dealt with the negative reaction to my proposals as best I could.

Edwards: That is very interesting. I did not have a good sense of that. Let me ask a related question. Years ago you said in an interview that one of the problems in dealing with Congress was that you made a lot of controversial proposals that asked a lot of Congress, frequently calling for members to face up to long-postponed issues. You listed several such issues when we began talking about your agenda.

Carter: Yes.

Edwards: And you said there was nothing in a lot of these issues for members of Congress. They were issues with no political benefit and they often called for facing some limits. So my question, which represents a perennial challenge that confronts all presidents, is how do you overcome parochial interests when there are no political benefits for members of Congress but you have to face these issues on the agenda because they are important for the nation?

Carter: I think that the overwhelming majority of members of Congress, maybe all of them, possess a sometimes-underestimated element of patriotism and a desire to do what is right for the country, even in the face of possible disapprobation at home. Some of them are highly idealistic and generous and willing to take a chance. Some of them have a very narrow ability.

I think that that is what the president has to tap. The president's ability to go to the local constituency directly, either through press conferences or through a visit to a state or bringing members to the White House, can help those reluctant members of Congress do what they may have already stated they knew was right for the country. That is the best answer I can give to you. If you go down the list of things that we achieved, it is hard for me to identify any that were politically popular. I mean, just look at them.

In 1980, I was the first Democratic presidential candidate that did not receive an overwhelming Jewish vote, because Israel gave up the Sinai and I talked about the Palestinian homeland. The Panama Canal treaties were devastating to me and to the members of the Senate. As I wrote in my book, there were twenty senators that voted for the treaties up for reelection in 1978. Only seven out of twenty came back to the Senate.

Two years later, there was almost an equal attrition rate, including Herman Talmadge here in Georgia. He lost his reelection although he had a sinecure. One of the major issues in the election was the Panama Canal treaties.

I think that those senators, including Russell Long and Herman Talmadge, voted for the Panama Canal treaties because they knew it was right. I think the general public underestimates the integrity, and the patriotism, and the political courage of the members of Congress.

Edwards: Mr. President, that is a wonderful, upbeat note on which to end. I thank you again for the opportunity to interview you.

Carter: I've enjoyed it. The hour has passed very rapidly.

Edwards: Yes, it just flew by.

Jimmy Carter: "We Never Dropped a Bomb. We Never Fired a Bullet. We Never Went to War."

Carole Cadwalladr / 2011

The Guardian, September 10, 2011. © Guardian News & Media Ltd.

Where does Jimmy Carter live? Well, close your eyes and imagine the kind of house an ex-president of the United States might live in. The sort of residence befitting the former leader of the most powerful nation on earth. Got it? Right, now scrub that clean from your mind and instead imagine the sort of house where a moderately successful junior accountant and his family might live.

It's what in America is called a "ranch house," or, as we'd say, a "bungalow." There are no porticoes. No columns. No sweeping lawns. There's just a small brick single-story structure that Jimmy and his wife, Rosalynn, built on Woodland Drive back in 1961 when he was a peanut farmer and she was a peanut farmer's wife, right in the heart of the town in which they grew up. Though Plains, Georgia, is barely a town. A street, might be a more accurate description. A single road going nowhere much.

At the end of the drive there's a fleet of black suburbans, giant SUVs with blacked-out windows: not too many junior accountants would have a crack team of secret service agents on site, it's true. But it's hard to overstate how modest it is. It's not much of an exaggeration to say that the whole thing would fit comfortably into the sitting room of just one of Tony and Cherie Blair's nine houses.

If you're under forty, you may not even remember Jimmy Carter. But you might recall President Bartlet from *The West Wing*. When I chat to Phil Wise, vice president of the Carter Center—the foundation Carter set up after leaving office—he reminds me that Martin Sheen partly based his character on Carter. Wise grew up next door to the Carter family, and as a college student he volunteered for the governor's campaign alongside Chip, the middle son. He worked for the presidential campaign "as the youngest gopher," and ended up in the White House as Carter's appointment secretary. (His character in *The West Wing*? "The African American man who sits outside the president's office.")

Was Carter really like President Bartlet? I ask Wise that question as we drive from the Carter Center in Atlanta to Plains through the rolling Georgian countryside, passing signs for catfish buffets and churches that exhort us to "Get out of Facebook and into God's Book." He considers the question seriously: "They were both former governors. Could both be very stubborn. And they both had a certain moral tone." He concludes: "There was a lot of Carter in the part."

In Britain we assumed that a politician that upright, that pure, could only be fictitious, and the expenses scandal has only reinforced that. But everything about Jimmy Carter's life—what he did as president, and what he's done since—has proved that "certain moral tone." And his home somehow encapsulates this. Inside, there's no hallway, just a patch of carpet separating a small dining room from a tiny sitting room. Then, all of a sudden, there's Jimmy.

Strictly speaking, he's still Mr. President, but it's hard to give the office its true gravitas in what looks like my mum's living room. And there's a plain, homespun quality about him that's reminiscent of that other great Jimmy, the patron saint of small-town American life: Jimmy Stewart. He'll turn eighty-seven in October, and is recovering from having both his knees replaced this summer, but the dazzling smile that once captivated America is still there. Though it's a terrible cliché, not to mention patronizing and ageist, to describe any octogenarian as "twinkly," he undeniably is.

He leads me slowly into the family room at the back of the house. Photographs of the children, grandchildren, and great grandchildren line the walls, and an old throw covers an even older sofa. Mary, the housekeeper who's been with the family for forty-odd years, brings Carter coffee in an ancient plastic cup, so old that the "Royal Caribbean" logo on it has faded nearly clean away. (Mary first came to work at the governor's mansion as a convicted murderer on day release, and—how's this for living your liberal beliefs?—the Carters asked her to look after their three-year-old daughter, Amy.)

It's a tiny place, Plains, two-and-a-half hours' drive from Atlanta, but there was never any doubt that Jimmy and Rosalynn would come home. "Oh no. Never. My folks have been here since 1860. And Rosalynn's folks since the 1830s, so our families have been involved with the Plains community for a long time. Our land is here, and our churches are here, and the schools that we went to are here. We have a full life here. No matter what we do around the world—and we now have programs in maybe seventy countries—we can work from here as easily as anywhere. This is where we've always come back to."

It was even more of a political Siberia in the pre-Internet age of 1981 when they first returned after Carter was defeated by Ronald Reagan. Wise came with them as their chief of staff. He recalls: "I was horrified when they said they were coming back here. I had to go and live with my parents. I thought they'd at least go to Atlanta." Thirty years on, the Carters are still incredibly involved with the town. I stay in the Plains Inn, a former funeral parlor turned into a hotel—and decorated by Rosalynn—at the Carters' instigation a few years back. One of my fellow guests works for the national park service at Carter's childhood home, now a museum, and tells me that the Carters still pop by to pick vegetables from the garden. And on most Sundays Jimmy wanders down to the Maranatha Baptist Church to teach Sunday school.

In the Carters' family room there's a Harry Potter book on the coffee table. At Christmas they're taking the entire family to the Wizarding World of Harry Potter at Universal Studios in Florida, and "so I thought I ought to acquaint myself with Harry Potter first," he says. He's never been one to skimp on the homework. Wise tells me: "My entire life, I've only ever managed to tell him one thing he didn't already know. I told him about how in the Second World War the Japanese tried to develop a folding airplane, and he said, 'I did not know that.' And I swear that's the only time that has ever happened."

Jimmy's early years on the family farm just outside Plains colored his entire life. As a boy during the Great Depression, he recalls, "streams of tramps, or we called them hobos, walked back and forth in front of our house, along the railroad." Even more influentially, it was a mostly Black community. "I learned at first hand the deprivation of both white and Black people living in a segregated community, which was then not challenged at all." Except by his own mother; thanks to her liberalism all his earliest playmates were Black.

Politics was never on the agenda. He's adamant about this, and when Rosalynn joins us she's bemused at the idea that he had any desire to be president when she married him.

"Oh no. I assumed he'd be in the navy and I'd be a naval wife. And he did too."

What would you have made of it had you known?

"I'd have thought it was tremendously exciting," she says.

"But ridiculous," he interjects.

"But totally ridiculous," she agrees.

They're not a couple, one senses, to shy away from stating bald truths. She's four years her husband's junior, and his equal in no-holds-barred energy. Until his knee operations temporarily prevented him, he swam "at least" forty lengths a day. And she does two-and-a-half miles around the property on a trike. They travel all over the world. And Peggy, who works for the Carter Center in Plains, tells me: "Every minute of every day is scheduled. They make us mere mortals look bone idle."

They're also—rather amazingly, given that they've just celebrated their sixty-fifth wedding anniversary—still as soppy about each other as two lovebirds. Everyone tells me this. Wise, four employees at the Carter Center, a man in a shop in Plains. And Jimmy and Rosalynn themselves. "They hold hands all the time," says Kelly Callahan, the assistant director of the Carter Center's health program. "They're just so cute. It's unbelievable. They do everything together. They come to all the staff meetings, and he'll always say, 'Did I forget anything, Rosalynn?'"

The story of Jimmy Carter's rise to power is, even thirty-five years on, still extraordinary. He truly was the man from nowhere. What was it, I ask Rosalynn, that enabled him to achieve the highest office in the land?

"Well, he was elected governor after a long campaign," she begins.

He interrupts her. "But what do you think propelled me from Plains to the White House?"

"Well, it was not until you were governor that you ever dreamed of being president, I don't think." And she continues in this vein until he interrupts her again.

"I'd be interested in hearing your answer to the question she asked," he says. And he really is. He's genuinely amused, and anticipating her potential reply. I get the sense she's not one to carelessly drop extraneous compliments. And eventually, after I rephrase it, she answers: "Well, I think he was always just looking for something more to do. In the navy he always got the best job, and always went one step up, and then another step. And I think it's in his nature to be adventurous. He's always said, 'If you don't try something, you won't succeed.' So he's never been afraid of failure."

It's not the most glowing of encomiums, all things considered, but he seems just about satisfied with this.

The thing you have to remember about Jimmy Carter, explains Steven Hochman, a Jefferson scholar who's worked with him for the past thirty years, helping research his books, is that he's a problem-solver by nature.

"He's very independent. If you grow up on a farm, you have to do things for yourself. When some problem comes up, he's used to solving it. His dad would do it. He would do it."

The young Jimmy studied engineering at the US naval academy in Annapolis, and even now he's drawn to practical problems he believes he can solve. The Carter Center, the foundation he and Rosalynn set up to promote and champion human rights, has been quietly working towards eradicating some of the world's nastier diseases. Guinea worm, a debilitating parasite, affected 3.5 million people worldwide when the Carter Center decided to try to eradicate it. Last year there were just 1,797 cases, mostly in South Sudan, and it looks set to be only the second (after smallpox) disease ever eliminated. Also on their hit list is river blindness, trachoma, and lymphatic filariasis, otherwise known as elephantiasis. As part of their human-rights efforts, they monitor elections in some of the most troubled corners of the world. "Our basic principle that has shaped us ever since we were founded is that we don't duplicate what other people do," says Carter. "If the World Bank or Harvard University or whoever is adequately taking care of a problem, we don't get involved. We only try to fill vacuums where people don't want to do anything."

Kelly Callahan calls the diseases "low-hanging fruit." "All the money goes to the big three: HIV, AIDS, and malaria. Everything else gets neglected. But these diseases [those the Center targets] affect the poorest of the poor. And by eliminating them we can make a huge difference to the lives of the poorest people on earth. I think he was drawn to this work because he likes projects that are outcome-orientated, and that are community-based—very much like he is. And he still asks all these questions. There's a desire to do more. A lot of us in this line of work are competitive. We want to do more. And he's like that. He's very passionate and intense."

And he shows no sign of letting up. He travels to the world's most intractable trouble spots as part of his work with the Elders, a group of elder statesmen (the caped crusaders of conflict resolution!) led by Nelson Mandela. In April he was in North Korea, trying again to negotiate an agreement on its nuclear program—as he did successfully in 1994 when he persuaded Kim Il-sung to agree to a nuclear weapons freeze. And this autumn he'll be in Haiti, helping build one hundred homes with volunteers from Habitat for Humanity, something he's done every year for the past thirty years. He's pioneered a model of postpresidential activism that Bill Clinton (or even ex-CEOs such as Bill Gates) have striven to emulate. And in 2002 he received the ultimate recognition for it: the Nobel Peace Prize.

Jimmy Carter approached his career with all the pragmatism of a practical man, and the deep-rooted morality of a religious one. American politics is increasingly dominated by what's called the religious right: conservatives who share an antiscientific world view, who treat evolution as a heretical theory, and universal healthcare as dangerous socialism. But Carter was of the religious left, a very different beast. He has a profound faith, rooted in his Baptist upbringing. He and Rosalynn read the Bible to each other every night and have done so for "thirty-something years." (They read in Spanish, so that they can practice their language skills at the same time; they're relentless self-improvers.) "I read a chapter one night," says Rosalynn. "And he reads a chapter the next night."

Politics wasn't so much a life choice he made, as the culmination of a sequence of events. "I was the chairman of the school board, and I was concerned about the public school system," he tells me. "I served as governor for as long as the constitution would permit me, and after that I ran for president in 1975. As you probably know, I was elected."

I heard, I say. Was there really never a master plan?

"Not at all. It was always just the next step. When I told my mother I was running for president, she said, 'president of what?'"

Ah yes, Miss Lillian. I've read about her. She was the great egalitarian influence of his childhood years: "She never treated our Black neighbors any differently than she did white people, and she was able to get away with that in a segregated society because she was a member of the medical profession [a nurse] and she was a very strong-willed woman anyway."

At the age of sixty-eight she went off to be a Peace Corps volunteer. There's a template, then, for an active old age, and he's started to resemble her in other ways too. He was the first high-profile figure to call for Guantánamo to be closed. He has criticized President Obama for failing to live up to his promises, for backtracking on foreign affairs, for failing to keep his resolve on Israel. ("When he said no more settlements, that was a major step forward. But then he backed away from that, as he's backed away from all of his other demands.")

But his name is being increasingly linked with Obama's in other contexts too. In the heavyweight journal *Foreign Policy*, Walter Russell Mead coined a phrase to characterize what he suggested was hampering President Obama's presidency: the Carter Syndrome. The "conflicting impulses influencing how this young leader thinks about the world threaten to tear his presidency apart. And in the worst scenario turn him into a new Jimmy Carter."

Or, as Nicholas Dawidoff put it in a major profile *Rolling Stone* published of Jimmy Carter this spring, it's because of Obama's "scattered ambitions, his lack of a grand vision, his outsider's discomfort with the ways of Washington, his fumbling economic policies . . . and above all his supposed lack of toughness, [that] the man he is increasingly compared with is Carter."

But as Dawidoff points out, Jimmy Carter is to Republicans what George W. Bush is to Democrats: their very names make their enemies foam at the mouth. And the reassessment is working both ways. For years Carter was considered a failure because he was a single-term president, because he was perceived as weak, and because he refused to take action against America's newly minted enemy, Iran. But, at this distance, the three great achievements of that single term seem even more of an achievement today: he forced through the Camp David Accords, one of only two peace treaties that Israel has ever signed, isolating Anwar Sadat and Menachem Begin at Camp David for thirteen days until he gradually wore them down; he also forced through the Panama Canal Treaty, a deeply unpopular move that returned the canal to Panama, but which prevented, many believe, a difficult and nasty war in Latin America; and he brought in an energy policy that saw him reduce America's dependency on imported oil by half. He was mocked—three decades before global warming became a fashionable concern—for walking around the White House, turning down the thermostats.

What he's most proud of, though, is that he didn't fire a single shot. Didn't kill a single person. Didn't lead his country into a war—legal or illegal. "We kept our country at peace. We never went to war. We never dropped a bomb. We never fired a bullet. But still we achieved our international goals. We brought peace to other people, including Egypt and Israel. We normalized relations with China, which had been nonexistent for thirty-something years. We brought peace between US and most of the countries in Latin America because of the Panama Canal Treaty. We formed a working relationship with the Soviet Union."

It's the simple fact of not going to war that, given what came next, should be recognized. "In the last fifty years now, more than that," he says, "that's almost a unique achievement." He was bitterly opposed to both Iraq wars. "Iraq was just a terrible mistake. I thought so in Iraq 1, and I was against it in Iraq 2." And it's not just George W. Bush who has blood on his hands, he says, but Tony Blair too: "I don't know what went on in private meetings when Tony Blair agreed to it. But had Bush not gotten that tacit support from Blair, I don't know if the course of history might have been different."

It's the second time we've talked about Blair. Money has disfigured American politics, Carter says. I ask him about the pledge he made the day after he lost his bid for reelection, when he told the press he would not make money off the back of his presidency. Is that true?

"That is correct," he says. Then he jokes: "It was kind of a weak moment." What inspired it?

"My favorite president, and the one I admired most, was Harry Truman. When Truman left office, he took the same position. He didn't serve on corporate boards. He didn't make speeches around the world for a lot of money."

Unlike Blair, I say. He's made a fortune since leaving office.

"I know he has. I know that."

What do you think of that?

"I wouldn't comment on that."

But then he doesn't need to. His whole life has been a comment on that.

It seems an impossibly long time ago, 1980. Prince Charles had just started dating Lady Diana Spencer. *Dallas* was the most popular TV show on both sides of the Atlantic. And Iran had recently been convulsed by the world's first Islamic revolution. More pertinent to the story of Jimmy Carter, Islamist students and militants had stormed the American embassy in Tehran in November 1979 and taken fifty-two members of staff hostage.

What could the US do? How could it save the hostages? It was a question that President Carter wrestled with for 444 long days. It paralyzed the presidency. Carter refused to campaign for reelection, refused to light the White House Christmas tree, refused to bomb Tehran.

Rosalynn has been quoted as saying that, had her husband bombed Tehran, he would have been reelected. I put this to Carter. "That's probably true. A lot of people thought that. But it would probably have resulted in the death of maybe tens of thousands of Iranians who were innocent, and in the deaths of the hostages as well. In retrospect I don't have any doubt that I did the right thing. But it was not a popular thing among the public, and it was not even popular among my own advisers inside the White House. Including my wife."

Really?

"Well, she thought I ought to be more willing to use military power."

Instead, he launched Operation Eagle Claw and, in a terrible confluence of extreme circumstances involving a sandstorm in the desert and a helicopter crash, eight US servicemen were killed. And no hostages were rescued. It was a humiliating failure. A failure his political career never recovered from.

Nicholas Schmidle, in his *New Yorker* account of the covert Seals mission that killed Osama bin Laden in May this year, notes that: "Deploying four

Chinooks was a last-minute decision made after President Barack Obama said he wanted to feel assured that the Americans could 'fight their way out of Pakistan.'" In the event they weren't needed (although the prime helicopter did crash in Bin Laden's compound and had to be abandoned), but the source of his anxiety is easy to guess. If there is one thing President Carter wishes he'd done differently, it would be sending "one more helicopter."

"We had to have six to bring back the hostages. We planned on seven. At the last minute I ordered eight. And, incredibly, three of them were decommissioned. One turned back to the aircraft carrier. One went down in a sandstorm in the desert, and the other had a hydraulic leak and crashed. Complete surprise to all of us, particularly to the military experts. We lost three out of eight helicopters. So then we had to withdraw. But if I'd had one more helicopter we could have brought back our hostages, and I would have been looked upon as a much more successful president."

Does that haunt you?

"Not really. I feel quite at ease with what we were able to do while I was president and what we've done since then."

No regrets?

"Not really. On balance, my life has been a constant stream of blessings rather than disappointments and failures and tragedies. I wish I had been reelected. I think I could have kept our country at peace. I think I could have consolidated what we achieved at Camp David with a treaty between Israel and the Palestinians. But I left office, and a lot of things changed. I think we would have had a very successful energy policy in this country and maybe around the world if I'd stayed in office. But that's just dreaming. I'm willing to accept that."

But it's a tantalizing prospect—to play alternative histories. To do a Jimmy Stewart with Jimmy Carter. The great what-might-have-been? Lots of different people tell me that the Middle East is his "unfinished business." Including him. "My constant prayer, my number one foreign goal, is to bring peace to Israel. And in the process to Israel's neighbors."

The Camp David Accords were a massive political gamble. He risked failure, but he succeeded where no one has before or since. In 2006 he published a book, *Palestine: Peace not Apartheid*, that excited fury from the American right. Steven Hochman tells me: "He's used to criticism. But I think it did hurt him. Some friends broke with him." And yet it's hard in Britain to understand what's so controversial about the book. He recommends, as has pretty much everybody else who's ever considered the situation, a two-state solution.

What about death? That's what I want to ask, but it's a bald question to ask anyone, let alone a former president who's accelerating towards his nineties. Wise splutters when I start talking about "your time left." I'd read, though, that Carter's favorite poet is Dylan Thomas, and he confirms this. So I ask: "Does the poem 'Do Not Go Gentle into That Good Night' have increasing resonance as you get older?"

"It does. It does," he says.

It's one of Thomas's most famous works, written as his father lay dying. He exhorts him instead to "rage, rage against the dying of the light." No one, not the wise, nor the good, nor even the wild men, he writes, has ever done enough to be ready to die.

Does he think he'll rage against the dying of the light? "I do, I do," he says. "Come on, I'll show you my Dylan Thomas." He takes me off to his study—a converted carport—where there's a whole row of Thomas and on the wall a carefully transcribed handwritten framed copy of "A Refusal to Mourn the Death, by Fire, of a Child, in London." "Amy did that for me," he says. "When she was a child." (The former first daughter was eight when she entered the White House, grew into a student firebrand and is now a stay-at-home mother in Atlanta: Rosalynn shows me a photo of Amy's elder son holding a baby and says, "I just love that photo. You know, I didn't have her until I was forty, and she's just had a baby in her forties.")

Does that poem also have special significance too for Jimmy?

"Not really," he says. "I just always really loved the sound of the words. It's so beautiful. I made all my children learn it by heart."

He's published his own poetry, too, along with many volumes of memoirs and a children's book. On the way out of the room he points out his oil paintings. Some are more successful than others (he got round the tricky self-portrait issue by painting himself from behind) but he's nothing if not a trier.

Karin Ryan, director of the human-rights program at the Carter Center, says what she loves about him is "that he's not jaded. He's not cynical. He gets exasperated but he still has hope. He gets enthusiastic in a very young way. There's almost an activist spirit about him."

She has worked at the Carter Center for more than twenty years after happening to visit the museum. "I saw the exhibits on Camp David and Panama and was blown away. I just thought: this is the way that American power should be. It was at the height of Reaganism, and I really related to this case of America as a moral power. Of using our power and institutions for peace and empowerment. Those of us who've stayed, we've hung around because we love them, Jimmy and Rosalynn."

Just not as much as they love each other. I find myself wondering about this. I've read Ronald Reagan's diaries and observed how much he doted on Nancy; and Laura Bush's memoirs, in which there's no doubt that her marriage to Dubya is a strong and happy one; as, surely, is Barack and Michelle's. A rock-solid marriage is almost a precondition of being elected president, it seems. But of all of them, none can match Jimmy and Rosalynn.

I mention to Carter how Kelly Callahan had spoken of him as a true romantic. Jimmy and Rosalynn both answer at once.

"I think he's romantic," says Rosalynn.

"I think so," says Jimmy, and he turns to look at her. "We're still very much in love. We miss each other when we're apart."

"That's why he doesn't like for me to go off on my own. I go sometimes but he doesn't like it. He likes for me to be at home."

Carter tells me he could never have become president without Rosalynn. "That is literally true. I was completely unknown, and I didn't have any money. So I went to one state and Rosalynn went to a different state. My oldest son and his wife, my middle son and his wife, my youngest son and his wife, my mother, and my mother's sister all went to different places every week. And they all campaigned for me. So by the time the other more famous candidates woke up, they'd already lost."

And their secret to a happy marriage? "We give each other space," says Rosalynn. "That's really important. And it was most important after we came home from the White House because we'd never been at home all day together every day. And it was a difficult time."

They've always made a point of learning new things together. They have their Spanish lesson once a week. They climbed mountains, learned how to fly fish, went birdwatching. "I learned how to ski when I was fifty-nine and Jimmy was sixty-three," says Rosalynn.

He was dating Miss Georgia Southwestern College when they first went out. Carter explains: "The next-to-last night that I was home on vacation from the naval academy, the whole family had a family reunion, and she [the beauty queen] couldn't have a date with me. So I was looking for a blind date, and picked up Rosalynn in front of the Methodist church."

Rosalynn takes up the story: "His sister, Ruth, was my best friend, and we'd been trying to get me together with him all summer. That night, Ruth and her date stopped in front of the church and picked me up, and I finally got to go with him."

So young Jimmy wasn't sad to see the back of the beauty queen?

"Well . . . after I'd had a date with Rosalynn, I was not interested in anybody else."

It was love at first sight?

"It was. For me."

I should be asking him for his views on Michele Bachmann. Or Binyamin Netanyahu. Or Kim Jong-il. But it's terribly affecting, watching and listening to them both together. And if President Obama does turn out to have the "Carter Syndrome," he might just need to count his blessings. I'm really not sure they make politicians like Jimmy Carter anymore. If they ever did.

President Carter

Ted Simons / 2015

Arizona Public Broadcasting, September 7, 2015.

Ted Simons: Coming up next on this special edition of *Arizona Horizon*, an interview with former president Jimmy Carter. We'll hear about President Carter's life, his political career and his new book. President Jimmy Carter, next on *Arizona Horizon*.

Arizona Public Broadcasting: *Arizona Horizon* is made possible by contributions from the Friends of Eight, members of your Arizona PBS station. Thank you.

Simons: Good evening, and welcome to this special edition of *Arizona Horizon*, I'm Ted Simons. President Jimmy Carter went from life in rural Georgia to military service and made a living as a farmer all before he got into politics, a career path that took him all the way to the White House as America's thirty-ninth chief executive. President Carter is in Phoenix promoting his new book, appropriately titled *A Full Life: Reflections at Ninety*. Joining us now is President Jimmy Carter. Good to have you, welcome to "Arizona Horizon."

Jimmy Carter: Good day to you and people all around Arizona.

Simons: It's great to have you. Thank you. Speaking of Arizona, thoughts, memories, and experiences in Arizona?

Carter: Just a beautiful state, and I campaigned here and forty-nine other states as a matter of fact. I had fairly good support here during the primary. In the general election I would say President Ford carried most of the states west of the Mississippi and I carried almost all of them east of the Mississippi, and I came out a little bit ahead.

Simons: You did. As far as the book is concerned, you've written a lot of books, you've written a number of them. Much of what's in this book has been touched on in some way shape or form in the previous efforts. How does this book differ from the others?

Carter: This is my twenty-ninth book. I've covered things in this book that I haven't really done before. Why I decided to run for president, for instance, my life in the Navy. The relationship I had with former presidents and ones that served after me. The things that I was able accomplish and resolve fully when I was president, and things that I had to postpone for others to address. Those kinds of things. My relationships with my wife early on, some of the major lessons I've learned in life and sometimes the hard way, which may be helpful to other people that read the book. A lot of things in there that I have never written before.

Simons: And indeed, *Reflections at Ninety*. Memories, what memories do you find at this stage, that you find that you enjoy most?

Carter: The most enjoyable part of my life has been since I left the White House. Of course, it was great to be president of the greatest country in the world and to have that authority and that power and influence and knowledge of internal affairs and that sort of thing. But I've had a much better life I would say during the thirty-five or so years since we left the White House. We have programs in seventy different countries in the world, and we deal with the most intricate matters that—governments don't want to fool with. We go to Myanmar, we go to meet with all the Palestinian groups, we go to North Korea, we go to Cuba, we go to Sudan and so forth, we go to Nepal—we meet with people that cause problems in the world that we can help resolve. We also have started a program of bringing people to—we just finished our hundredth troubled election in May. And this year we'll treat about seventy-one million people so they won't go blind or have some other horrible disease that is no longer known in an even halfway developed world, but it afflicts hundreds of millions in the very poor countries, particularly in Africa and Latin America.

Simons: Getting so much done now after leaving the White House. Why do you think it's working better? The best memories sound like they are the most recent ones for you. Why do you think that is?

Carter: Because I was president first. I wouldn't be able to do the things that I know how to do now, if I hadn't been president of a great country first. And I wouldn't have the direct access to any leader on earth. Any king or president or prime minister that I want to meet, I just call them and he's very eager to meet me. Then I tell them what we want to do in his country or her country, and they generally agree and cooperate with us. If I go to a pharmaceutical company and ask them for hundreds of millions of doses of medicine. Primarily because I have been president of a country and they respect me, they give this medicine to us and we can go into the jungle areas and cities and towns—and also in the desert areas and give medicine to people. I couldn't orchestrate honest and fair election processes in troubled countries, and actually go in with some associates and conduct an honest and fair election, if it hadn't been for my White House experience. And my wife and I also, every year for one week, we go and build Habitat houses for poor people in need. We've done that now for thirty-two years. Later on this year we'll be in Nepal where Mount Everest is; we're building one hundred houses for one week with other volunteers who will join us. Those are the kind of things I was able to do primarily because I was president.

Simons: What memories for you are the hardest?

Carter: Well, the White House years are the most troubling. The last year I was in office was when the hostages were being held; Iran was the most troubling of all. I prayed more about it, I was in more concern about it. But we eventually brought every hostage home safe and free, and I protected the interests of my country, but that was a very trying time. And then we had some very intense negotiations to formalize relations with the People's Republic of China for instance, to start ending apartheid in African countries, and to go to Panama and resolve the issue of the Panama Canal treaties. To go to the Holy Land and bring peace with Israel and Egypt, those were some of the things that were challenging to me.

Simons: You said it was great to be president.

Carter: It was.

Simons: Did you enjoy being president?

Carter: I did, yes. There were some trying times and I would say the overwhelming joyous and productive and exciting and challenging, and unpredictable, adventurous times have been since I left the White House, because of the diversity of the things we do, and the direct personal contact we make. We go into individual villages and assess their problems in health care, and then we actually administer medicines if it's needed, or teach them how to resolve an ancient problem that people may have suffered for 20,000 years. That's very gratifying to us.

Simons: It's interesting, you talk about all the things you're doing and the Carter Center is doing, and moderating elections, monitoring elections, getting health care to people that need it. Such an active public service kind of a life. Yet, there you are in rural Georgia as a kid marrying the girl—you literally married the girl next door, didn't you?

Carter: I did. As a matter of fact my mother was a nurse. The first day Rosalynn was alive I went over and looked through the cradle at my future wife, my mother tells me. We still live in the same little town, about 650 people, Plains, Georgia.

Simons: You write that most of your friends were African American.

Carter: Almost all of them.

Simons: When did the racial divide, the racial question, when did that hit you? At what age?

Carter: When I was younger I didn't have any friends except Black boys and girls. My mother was a registered nurse, she was gone a lot. So African American women kind of took care of me and raised me and taught me about a proper attitude toward life, toward God, my fellow human beings and taught me the names of trees and birds and things. I was raised in a Black culture. I would say when I was about fourteen years old—I wrote a poem about this called "A Pasture Gate." Two African American friends and I we were coming out of a field to the barn and went through a gate. When they got to the gate they opened it and stepped back to let me go through first. I thought there was a trip wire and I would fall down. I finally realized later that that was a time in their life and mine when their parents probably told them, it's time for you to start treating Jimmy as a white person. And not as a complete equal with you anymore. As I said at the end of the poem, that was drawing a line between friends and friends, race and race. It was later that I realized that's probably what happened. Then I was in the submarine force, I was a submarine officer. When Harry Truman ordained as commander and chief, as president, that all the racial discrimination should be over in all the armed services and also the civil service of our government. And that was kind of a turning point in my life.

Simons: The pasture gate incident in the book is fascinating—you can see in the way you write it that it really did impact you.

Carter: Well, it did.

Simons: It was something you weren't aware of, and all of a sudden here's the world.

Carter: And I realized later that when we finally got the Civil Rights Act passed and Martin Luther King Jr., and Andy Young and Rosa Parks were successful, we had removed the millstone from around the neck of both Black and white people. I think the last few months with the tragedy in South Carolina and the abuse by police of Black people, that we are beginning to see that we still have a long way to go. That we kind of breathed a sigh of relief, said it's all over now, no more discrimination, all equality from now on, no more white supremacy. But that's not true yet.

Simons: Still have a ways to go.

Carter: Still have a ways.

Simons: Your father, you write, showed fairness and respect for all but he was a man of his time and place.

Carter: He was, and everybody else was, too. As was the Supreme Court, as was the US Congress, as were all the churches as were all the American Bar Association members. There was no question in those days of the 1930s and 1940s that racial discrimination was wrong and should be corrected.

Simons: You write quite a bit about your naval experience. How did the Navy shape your life?

Carter: I would say the preeminent fact at the naval academy was do not lie. If a midshipman there told a slightest falsehood, he was out. That was the end of his naval career. If you stepped on the grass and somebody saw you and you later said, I didn't step on the grass, you were gone. I think to tell the truth was a preeminent mandate, and I carried that over. Later it became kind of a motif for me. If I tell a lie, don't vote for me, and so forth. It was a time in history that we had had too many lies told by our government and too many devastating blows. The Watergate crisis, the Vietnam War, misrepresentations. And the assassinations of Martin Luther King Jr. and the Kennedy brothers. And the revelation by the Frank Church committee that the president and the CIA had committed crimes against you might say enemy leaders overseas. Those kinds of things were all revealed, and I came along at a right time.

Simons: You came at the right time, but you came along at a time when addressing these issues and doing it as a bit of an outsider—you were considered an outsider—

Carter: Oh, yeah.

Simons: Didn't make you many friends, did it?

Carter: No, but I didn't need many friends. I had about twelve opponents, all more famous than I was. And either big states or the US Senate or something like that. By the time I got recognized as a legitimate candidate, all of the—you might say the semiprofessional politicians around different states had already aligned themselves with more favored candidates. So I had to take what was left over, young people and newcomers to politics. I didn't have any money, we didn't have money at all. And we didn't ever stay in a hotel room. We just got people to let us stay in their house if we could beg them to, or we slept in an automobile. That was all my staff. When I ran finally against Gerald Ford, who was an incumbent president, he and I raised zero money. We didn't raise a single dollar of contribution from anybody that might want something back after we were elected. And the same thing happened by the way four years later when I ran against Ronald Reagan. We didn't raise any money. We just took a $1 per person check that some taxpayers volunteered to give.

Simons: When you see what happens in this day and age, regarding money and politics, I think you write that you consider it legal bribery.

Carter: It is legal bribery. There's no doubt, you can't possibly hope to be the Democratic or Republican nominee for president if you can't raise two or $300 million. I won't condemn those people that want to give. But some of them want something back after the election is over, either from an incumbent president or congressman or US senator or governor or something like that. It's made it completely legally to give unlimited amounts and get something in return. That's one of the main reasons we've seen such a dramatic change in the relationship between very rich people who are getting richer and richer and the average working people in this country that are not.

Simons: The campaign against President Ford was different, as well, you were both respectful of each other. And that respect lasted really after you both left the White House.

Carter: Well, the historians said publicly and in writing that the two former presidents of the United States that had the closest personal friendship was Gerald Ford and me. I was very proud of that. His wife was a friend of my wife and the children were friends of each other. So we had a very intimate and gratifying relationship.

Simons: As far as being in the White House, you write that you had problems with the media. I think almost every president says they have problems with the media. You thought maybe they couldn't accept a southerner, that that was a factor at play. Talk to us about that.

Carter: When I was elected, I was the first person from the Deep South chosen that was chosen to be president in about 150 years. It just wasn't a thing done. I think a lot of the media from the North, they controlled the media pretty much, felt there was some power behind my background or an inclination towards racism, that I was a southerner that was still committed to racial distinctions. That was right after the Watergate revelations some investigating reporters had gotten famous because they revealed what went on with Richard Nixon. I think they thought they were going find something wrong with me that would be gratifying for their own career. I was in office forty-eight months, and forty-six months I had negative news coverage. Just the first two months was the only positive coverage. We learned to live with it.

Simons: Again, we hear from presidents afterwards or supporters of presidents, everyone seems to have a problem with the media, don't they?

Carter: That's true.

Simons: The Camp David accords were amazing. To think that in this day and age, you had Egypt and Israel shaking hands there and you right there. Those talks at Camp David were very personal, the relationships were very personal. I thought signing a photograph with Menachem Begin, I thought that was a fascinating story.

Carter: Well, we had failed at the end of twelve days. We were there thirteen and we were getting ready to go back to Washington and announce that we had not been successful. Begin was very angry with me because I had made some demands on Israel he didn't think he could accept. He asked me for a signed photograph of me and him and Sadat together just as a souvenir. My secretary called Israel and got the names of his eight grandchildren. So instead of putting "Best wishes, Jimmy Carter," I put "With love and best wishes to," and I put the name of each grandchild and his son. I took it over to his cabin to give to him. He was very cool toward me. He said, "Thank you, Mr. President." He reached out and took the photograph and turned around and walked away kind of. I stood there and he looked at the photographs and began to read the names of his grandchildren one by one. When he got to about the third name, he had tears coming down his cheeks and his voice was kind of choked up. I was too. He finally said, "Mr. President, why don't we make one more effort?" We made another effort and we were successful. But I think it was because of those photographs and his realization that he was possibly bringing peace to his own grandkids that he said, "I'll be a little more flexible."

Simons: Your most difficult political decision was the Panama Canal, but your most important diplomatic decision was China.

Carter: I think that's right, yes. Getting two thirds of the Senate to vote for the Panama Canal treaties was much more difficult for me than getting elected as president in the first place. It was one of the most courageous votes that the Senate ever did. There were twenty people in the Senate that voted for those treaties in 1978 that ran for reelection. Out of the twenty only seven came back the next January. That was very difficult, but I think as far as shaking up political alliances and the world on a sustained basis, my decision to normalize diplomatic relations with China was probably more significant.

Simons: Indeed. I also noticed you did have a health care plan and you had ideas there. But Teddy Kennedy of all people seemed to get in the way. What happened there?

Carter: Ted Kennedy wanted to be president. And for the last two years I was in office he was a full-time candidate against me. He didn't want me to experience any major successes, which I can certainly comprehend, having been in politics myself. But we worked on this comprehensive health plan for every human being, basically to extend Medicare to everybody. And we had all six committees in the House and Senate lined up to help us including Ted Kennedy's committee. In the last week when we were getting ready to reveal it, he changed his mind and decided to oppose it. He was powerful enough in the Senate to block its passage. There's no doubt we would have had comprehensive health care for all Americans thirty years earlier if Kennedy had maintained his commitment to the program that he had helped me develop.

Simons: Last year in office, we've got to get there, you write that it was the most stressful and unpleasant of your life.

Carter: It was.

Simons: As far as the hostages obviously. The failed rescue mission, was that the right decision? Regardless of 20/20 hindsight, your secretary of state Cyrus Vance did not think it was a good decision.

Carter: He was the only one.

Simons: And he wound up resigning, but do you think it was still the right decision?

Carter: It was, it was. We had to have six helicopters to bring out all the hostages and the rescue team. We couldn't have left them behind because they would have very likely been killed by the Iranians. And the military told me we need to have at least six helicopters come out. So I decided we'd have seven and an eighth. We had two helicopters go down, one turned back unexpectedly to the aircraft carrier. I don't know why yet. The other went down in a sandstorm which left us with six. In Desert 1 we were getting ready to go in and rescue we knew where everyone was and so forth. That particular helicopter had a fuel leak and swerved sideways and hit one of the airplanes there. And we had to abort the mission. So I think if we'd had one more helicopter we would have gotten the hostages out. I would have had a second term and history might have been a little bit better. But I don't think my life would have been much more pleasant. [*Laughter*]

Simons: You refrained from using the military against Iran. Why?

Carter: Well, I tried to promote two basic ideals of mine as a Christian. One was to keep the peace. We worship the Prince of Peace. And to promote human rights in all their aspects. I did the best I could not only to keep peace for my own country but to keep peace for others, including Egypt and

Israel. I would say most of my advisors, even including my wife, proposed that I should attack Iran militarily, which we could have destroyed Iran. I just decided to try to use peaceful means. I was fortunate, not only protecting my country's interests, but we never dropped a bomb, never launched a missile, never fired a bullet while I was in office. A lot was good fortune, a lot was commitment on my part.

Simons: The hostages were not released until after the election. There's been a lot written and speculated about this. I want to ask you. Do you think there was some sort of deal, do you think that was by design?

Carter: That's a question I never have been willing to answer. I deliberately avoided getting involved in any sort of research to prove it. There were books written about it that say there was a deal between the White House and the Ayatollah. I don't know. The only thing I know is I stayed up three days and nights I never went to bed even the last three days I was in office. I negotiated between Iran and twelve other countries to get the hostages freed. At 9:00 that morning of Inauguration Day when I was going out of office, all the hostages were in an airplane at the end of the runway ready to take off. I was waiting for them to take off and the Ayatollah didn't let them do so until five minutes after I was no longer in office. Why? I don't know.

Simons: Do you want to know?

Carter: Not really.

Simons: That incident, I know Kennedy and Reagan at the time, they called you an ineffective leader, they called you weak on that. Your emphasis on human rights, that was seen at the time as weakness. How did you respond to that? This was used against you and it worked; you did not win that reelection.

Carter: Well, I didn't use it wisely. I said in the book here, one of the things I didn't do was to keep the Democratic party vital and alive and loyal to me. I let Kennedy move in and he took over a good portion of the Democratic party, more ultra-liberal members. I had to depend on Republicans to help me get my legislation passed. Which I got, I got as much support from Republicans as I did Democrats when I was in the White House. I had a very good batting average. But I think the human rights issue was one of the strongest and politically demanding things that I did. Because we brought the freedom and peace to a lot of people on Earth that never had known it before. If you have time, I'll give you one quick example.

Simons: Please.

Carter: In Latin America, when I became president, we were in bed with every dictator in Latin America, in South America and in Central America and in the Caribbean. Whenever one of our dictator friends was challenged by Native Americans or native peoples, indigenous people, poor people, we would send troops down, either Marines or Army troops to defend our military friend, who probably graduated from West Point and his kids went through American colleges, but who also would provide us with very beneficial contracts for pineapple and bananas and bauxite and iron ore and those kinds of things. We had a lot of money flowing into us because we supported them. I put an end to that. And within seven years every country in South America had become a democracy. When before that almost every one of them was a dictatorship. I think that showed human rights paid off.

Simons: We're about to run out of time. I could talk to you forever. You have mentioned these are the best [years]—and I think at the end of your book you write that the life you have now is the best of all. And you have been talked about and people refer to you as the best former president we've ever had. Is that a little bittersweet to hear?

Carter: To my wife it is. It really doesn't bother me, you know. I did the best I could. As Chris Mondale said, we told the truth, we kept the law, and we kept the peace. We protected human rights. We did the best we could.

Simons: It's been an absolute pleasure having you here. The book was very interesting. I was around back then, as well, and it brings back a lot of memories. Congratulations on a life well lived. Do you ever just press the snooze button and say, "I feel like sleeping in?" You're a busy man.

Carter: Well, we do. We stay busy but also enjoy life very much. We have thirty-eight in our family now, twenty-two grandchildren and great-grandchildren. I met with some in Los Angeles when I was there recently. So we have a good quiet life, my wife and I do in Plains, but we still have eighty countries around the world we visit whenever we can.

Simons: My goodness. President Carter, great to have you here. Thank you so much.

Carter: Thoroughly enjoyed it, good questions.

Simons: Thank you. That is it for now, I'm Ted Simons. Thank you so much for joining us. You have a great evening.

Index

About the Editor

Tom Head, PhD, is author or coauthor of more than three dozen nonfiction books on a wide range of topics, including University Press of Mississippi's *Conversations with Carl Sagan* (2006). He lives and works in downtown Jackson, Mississippi, where he serves as chaplain for several nonprofit organizations.

CPSIA information can be obtained
at www.ICGtesting.com
Printed in the USA
JSHW020007230623
43651JS00003B/23